Fantasy Football for Smart People:

What the Experts Don't Want You to Know

Jonathan Bales, Writer at RotoWire

Table of Contents

Fantasy Football for Smart People: What the Experts Don't Want You to Know answers 25 of the most pressing fantasy football questions to help take your team over the edge.

Preface

In the summer of 2012, I published a book called *Fantasy Football for Smart People: How to Dominate Your Draft*. That book—an in-depth "philosophy" of drafting (which is updated for this season, by the way)—was fairly popular and I had a blast writing it, so I decided to continue the series in 2013.

Fantasy Football for Smart People: What the Experts Don't Want You to Know has a different format than most other books. Instead of telling one continuous story, *What the Experts Don't Want You to Know* examines 25 critical questions in the world of fantasy football. Do running backs break down after seasons with a heavy workload? What's the best draft spot? How can you best project rookies? I wanted to know the answers to those questions and others, and I figured you might too. So I did my best to answer them.

The presentation of the book is a bit "Nietzschean" in that each section represents an independent thought. That means you can jump around as you'd like; while I build upon certain fundamental concepts, you don't necessarily need to read the book in the traditional front-to-back manner. If you're not particularly interested in a specific question, feel free to skip it. I urge you to come back to each section at some point, however, as the answers to even the most "obvious" of questions aren't always so straightforward.

As I did in *How to Dominate Your Draft*, I've added "The Bottom Line" to the end of each section. There, you can find bottom-line analysis that sums up the major points of the topic. If you don't completely follow all of the analysis pertaining to each question, "The Bottom Line" should provide some clarity.

In addition to this book, I also published *Fantasy Football for Smart People: How to Cash in on the Future of the Game*. The book is the first of its kind to break down the actual strategies used by the top owners in the world of weekly fantasy football. With weekly fantasy football growing at an exponential rate, there's a whole lot of money to be made, and advanced weekly owners are already cashing in to the tune of hundreds of thousands of dollars in profit. With input from one of the weekly fantasy football "sharks"—FFFC $150,000 winner Peter Jennings—*How to Cash in on the Future of the Game* will show you how to manage your money, select the perfect websites, make projections, and create lineups so that you can finally treat your hobby as you always wanted—as an investment.

I'm confident that all three books will be of use to you in 2013, aiding you in your path to either a championship or weekly league profits. If you find the books insightful and useful—even if it's a hard copy that you use to prop up a table—please consider checking out my 2013 draft guide, projections, rankings, and sleepers at

FantasyFootballDrafting.com. Many of the fantasy owners who used my rankings in 2012 ended up with C.J. Spiller, Doug Martin, Dez Bryant, and ~~Ryan Mathews~~, err...umm, just Spiller, Martin, and Bryant.

I'll also be posting much of my content at Fantasy Football Drafting throughout the year, so stop by to check it out. Thank you to everyone who made this book happen, including the guys at RotoWire, where some of my thoughts and essays first took form. Thanks for your support, and best of luck in 2013!

1 Which draft position is the most valuable?

In 2007, LaDainian Tomlinson was the first pick in fantasy drafts across the country. LT delivered in a big way that year, racking up 310 fantasy points even in standard leagues—28 more than second-place running back Brian Westbrook.

The 2007 season might not seem like anything special, but that was the last time the top overall fantasy selection ended the season No. 1 at his position (LT was really the third-best fantasy player that season, behind record-breaking years from Tom Brady and Randy Moss).

In the world of fantasy football, many of us are guilty of thinking we're superior prognosticators than we really are. The truth is that predicting the outcomes of something as complex as football is really, really tough, so it's no surprise that fantasy owners, even as a whole, are far from perfect.

But just how good (or bad) is the general public? What's the difference between the first draft position and the last, and what sort of return on investment might one expect with each? I wanted to answer those questions, so I spent some time tracking the relationship between fantasy draft slots and production. I included the top 20 picks from the past five seasons, analyzing fantasy points-per-game instead of overall points to correct for injuries that would throw off cumulative results.

Return on Investment for Top 20 Fantasy Picks: 2007-2012

A few points of interest:

- No. 1 picks—all running backs—have provided 82.7 percent of the production of the top player at their position. The low was Chris Johnson in 2010, who scored 70.7 percent as many points as top-scorer Arian Foster. Amazingly, three of the top four backs from 2010—Foster, Peyton Hillis, and Jamaal Charles—weren't drafted in the top 20.

- No. 2 selections—again all running backs—have returned 80.3 percent of the production of the top-scoring back. The high was Foster in 2011, who led the league

in fantasy points, and the low was Michael
Turner in 2009 at 63.3 percent.

- After the top two picks in fantasy drafts,
there has been a significant drop in
production. No. 3 picks have provided 71.4
percent of peak production, and No. 4
selections check in at just 65.0 percent.
- Taking first-round selections in isolation, it
appears superior to have a top two pick
over any other. After No. 2, there doesn't
appear to be much of a difference between
picks No. 3 and No. 12.
- The true "cutoff" of talent over the years
has been right around the 14/15 range.
Since 2007, No. 14 overall picks have
returned 72.4 percent of peak production.
That number drops to 64.3 percent for No.
15 selections.

In the traditional snake draft format, picking last in
the first round can be a good thing, because you also
acquire the first pick in the second round. Since No.
13 draft picks have provided a robust 78.3 percent of
peak production, the overall value of drawing the
final pick in the first round is boosted.

To examine which draft spot is really the most
advantageous, I combined the peak production
percentages for the first two rounds of a 12-team
league. After doing do, the value of the first two
draft spots disappeared. Since the number of elite

players has generally been around 14 per year, the last selections in a 12-team league have provided the most value. Those owners miss out on a truly top-tier talent, but they can still get their hands on two outstanding players.

Nonetheless, I'm not sure we can draw any ironclad conclusions just yet. Examining third and fourth-round picks could alter the results a bit. Further, we don't see much of a pattern in the data. The fluctuations in the results—the continual up-and-down that we see—makes it difficult to say which draft slots are inherently the "best." Is the No. 6 overall pick really that much better than the No. 7 overall selection? Probably not.

Ultimately, I think the value of each draft slot really depends on the year, but the data suggests that you don't need to panic if you're picking in the back of the first round; the 74.8 percent return for owners picking No. 12 overall is the highest mark of any draft slot in the past five years. With the increasing popularity of third-round reversal drafts in which the No. 12 overall pick selects first in both the second and third rounds, the value of the 12th draft spot soars even higher.

- **Draft Slot Consistency**

Of course, fantasy football isn't all about averages. It's useful to know the return provided by each draft slot, but it's just as useful to understand the consistency with which they provide that return. That is, we want to know not only how many points we can expect to receive from the players drafted in each spot, but also how likely they are to reach certain thresholds. A draft slot that returns 65 percent of peak production might be superior to one that returns 70 percent if the former can provide that 65 percent return very consistently.

In short, we want to know the "bust rate" associated with each draft slot. I tracked how often over the past five years each draft spot was able to provide two players with a 70 percent minimum return in the first two rounds.

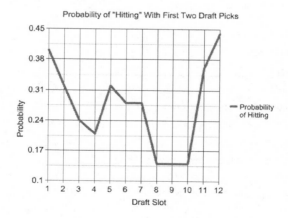

Probability of "Hitting" With First Two Draft Picks

Once again, the 12th pick has been the most profitable. Choosing from that slot, owners have been able to grab two players that have scored at least 70 percent of the points as the top players at their respective positions 44.9 percent of the time. That's the highest rate of any draft spot, with the No. 1 (and No. 24) overall selection coming in second at 40.0 percent.

In my original analysis on overall return, I argued that after the first two draft picks, there isn't much of a difference between picks No. 3 through No. 12. In terms of consistency, however, the results are a bit different. Since, 2007, owners selecting with the No. 3 overall pick have been able to draft two players with at least a 70 percent return almost 70 percent more often than owners choosing in the No. 8, No. 9, and No. 10 spots. In terms of consistency, the middle of the draft appears to be the worst place to be.

And there's a lot to be said about consistency. In the early rounds, owners should try to be as safe as possible, choosing players who are unlikely to be busts, even if it means sacrificing upside. The potential ceiling of the draft's highest picks is very small relative to the cost, so it's critical for owners to limit players' floors, i.e. draft conservatively.

Ultimately, the shrewdest owners are the ones who can manage to limit risk without dramatically decreasing upside. Thus, both return on investment and consistency are important factors in drafting. If we combine the results from both studies by adding the hit rate for each draft slot to the overall return of investment from the first two picks, we get the following results:

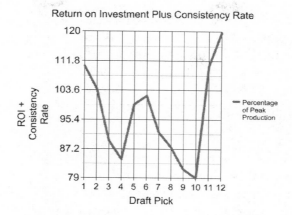

So what are we left with here? Which draft slot is the "best"? Although I think every season is different and the value of each draft pick is inherently fluid, there's definitely some value in choosing at either the top or bottom of the draft.

With either of the first two picks, you get consistency. You're almost guaranteed a top-level player, and that sort of "sure thing" isn't there after the first couple of picks. The extra advantage that comes with a late first-round pick is an early second-round pick. Since the drop-off of top-tier talent has historically been in the 13-14 range, it means you can grab two studs. When choosing in the middle of the first round, you have to forgo the consistency that accompanies the top two selections, but you don't reap the benefits of an early second-round pick.

- ## Another Advantage of a Late Pick

Drafting near the end of rounds (but not as the last pick in a round) can allow for a few advantages. If you are in a 12-team league and you are allowed to pick your own draft spot, consider that spots 2, 3, 4, 9, 10, and 11 might have more intrinsic value than 1, 5, 6, 7, 8, and 12.

In snake drafts that use a reverse draft order for subsequent rounds, drafting near the end of a round allows you to accurately predict which players might get selected between your own picks. If you hold the 11th and 14th overall picks in a 12-team league, for example, you could easily bypass specific players in favor of others if you know the sole owner drafting between you doesn't need or want the player you intend to draft in the later round.

For instance, assume your pick is approaching in the fifth round and you are considering a running back and a quarterback. Only one person picks behind you before the round is over, and he already has two running backs, but no quarterback. In such a situation, it is easy to see why you should select the signal- caller, even if the running back is higher on your board.

Drafting in the middle of rounds doesn't afford you this advantage. Yes, you don't need to wait nearly two full rounds to make selections as is the case when drafting at the edge of rounds, but it isn't possible to predict the players to be selected between any of your picks anyway.

When you combine the ability to make predictions regarding future picks with the historic data I provided, you can see why the second-to-last pick is a good place to be.

- ## The Bottom Line

The "best" draft slot changes each year, but in general, it's suitable to choose at either the beginning or end of the first round. In the middle, you won't get a truly elite player, but you also can't draft again until the middle of the second round. In leagues that use a third-round reversal draft format, the value of the last pick or two is even greater than in traditional formats. In those leagues, choosing second-to-last might be ideal.

2 Do running backs really break down after a heavy workload?

As a writer, one of my favorite things to do is dispel "truisms" that exist within the sport of football. "Never take points off of the board" and "you run to set up the pass" are two long-held beliefs that simply have no basis in reality. There are lots of times you should take points off of the board, and in today's NFL, teams really don't need an effective running game to win. Yeah, I said it.

In fantasy football, there are a plethora of "truisms" that many owners use as a basis for creating their rankings. "Wide receivers tend to break out in their third season" and "you can always wait on a quarterback" are two of the most popular.

Today, I'm going to take a look at the merits of avoiding running backs coming off of seasons with huge workloads. Many fantasy owners believe that, following seasons in which running backs touched the ball often, they tend to break down, often getting injured or seeing a decrease in effectiveness.

I researched the production of all running backs with 350 or more carries in a season.

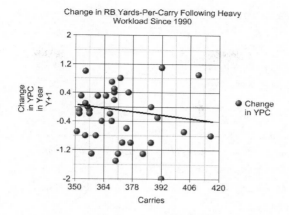

Change in RB Yards-Per-Carry Following Heavy Workload Since 1990

You can see that when running backs record 350-plus carries in Year Y, they generally see a decline in yards-per-carry in Year Y+1. Of the 37 running backs to generate 350 carries since 1990, 24 (64.9 percent) produced a lower YPC number in the following season. The average decline in YPC was 0.26 for all backs, 0.38 for the top 20 backs (in terms of workload), and an incredible 0.51 for the top 10 backs.

A decrease of 0.51 YPC from one season to the next is a pretty hefty number. At first glance, it really appears as though a high volume of carries can have adverse effects on a running back's subsequent season.

As with many things in fantasy football and life in general, looks can be deceiving. Whenever collecting stats, it is important to determine how representative the group is of the whole. If you poll 1,000 people regarding this year's presidential election, you'll get vastly different results if you perform one poll in the heart of Alabama and the other poll in Vermont.

When a group of stats isn't representative of the whole, it is known as a selection bias. A selection bias is at work when we analyze running backs coming off of seasons with heavy workloads, and it can lead us astray when making conclusions about those backs' future effectiveness.

For a running back to acquire 350 or more carries in a season, a lot of things need to go right. He needs to be healthy; it's simply a prerequisite for receiving so many touches. Of the 37 running backs who have gotten 350 carries in a season, the total number of games missed was five combined. Only five missed games out of a possible 592 played!

Secondly, the running back necessarily must maintain a certain level of efficiency. Without it, he won't keep acquiring so many touches. If Chris Johnson is averaging 2.0 YPC after eight games this year, for example, you can bet he won't be getting the ball nearly as much in the second half of the season. Of the top 15 running backs in single-season carries since 1990, only two have averaged less than 4.3 YPC. Nine of those 15 were above 4.5 YPC.

Knowing that the selection of backs with 350-plus carries in a season is naturally skewed toward those that were healthy and effective has profound implications on our conclusions. Naturally the outliers from the previous year, these backs are likely to regress toward the mean, independent of their workload. That is, running backs who have a high YPC are likely to regress in the following season whether they got 350 carries or 100.

That idea is supported by the stats. When examining the relationship between YPC in Year Y and Year Y+1 among all backs, we see a trend similar to that of the high-workload rushers alone.

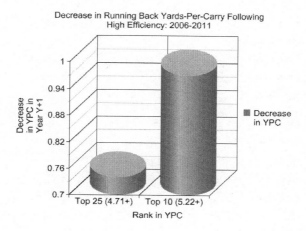

Decrease in Running Back Yards-Per-Carry Following High Efficiency: 2006-2011

You can see the dramatic decline in efficiency among the NFL's most effective runners over the past five years. Heavy workload or not, running backs coming off of seasons in which they recorded a high YPC almost always saw that number drop in the following year. Of the 25 backs to average 4.71 YPC (on at least 180 carries) from 2006 to 2010, only three (12.0 percent) increased their YPC in the next season. The average decline was an astounding 0.74 YPC. Of the 10 backs to average 5.22 YPC, the average decline was almost a full yard on each carry.

Ultimately, running backs coming off of seasons with lots of touches are likely to regress in terms of both efficiency and health, but that information is both insignificant and irrelevant to fantasy owners. Since high-carry running backs are outliers from the previous year, all you're really saying when claiming that "running backs with X carries in Year Y see a decrease in health and YPC in the following season" is that running backs with unusually good health and an abnormally high YPC are likely to have worse health and a lower YPC the next season. Yeah, duh.

Thus, while the production of a running back coming off a season with a heavy workload is likely to decrease, it is not a legitimate reason to avoid that player in fantasy drafts. The (probable) decrease in production is due to the previous season being a statistical outlier (a result that is unusually far from the mean).

The best way to look at the situation is this: what is the running back's chance of generating production that is comparable to the previous year? It is actually *the same* as it was prior to the start of the previous season, i.e. the workload has no noticeable effect on his ability to produce.

For example, if a running back has a 20 percent chance of garnering 2,000 total yards in a season, that percentage remains stable (assuming his skill level does the same) from year to year. Thus, the chance of this player following a 2,000 yard season with another is unlikely, but not due to a heavy workload (a necessity for such productive output), but rather the fact that he only had a 20 percent chance to do so from the start. We wrongly (and ironically) attribute the decrease in production to the player's prior success when, in reality, no such causal relationship exists.

- **The Bottom Line**

While it might seem risky to jump on a running back coming off of a high-volume season, don't be afraid. Actually, total touches is by far the most predictive stat for running back fantasy points; since running backs all see around the same overall efficiency, the best ones tend to be those with the most carries and receptions. That means not only should you not be downgrading workhorse running backs, but you should actually be jumping on them, regardless of size of their workload in the previous season.

3 How much does a great quarterback help a receiver?

No one in their right mind thinks Larry Fitzgerald has been an elite fantasy wide receiver because of his recent quarterback situation; rather, Fitzgerald excels in spite of the men throwing him the ball. All other things being equal, we obviously want to draft (and start) receivers with great quarterbacks.

In regards to average draft position, however, the issue becomes a little bit trickier. Since average draft position is a reflection of public opinion, we'd expect receivers without standout passers to drop in the rankings. Dwayne Bowe is a big-time receiver, for example, but got selected just 22nd in 2012 fantasy drafts because many believed the combined passer rating of Matt Cassel and Brady Quinn would probably equal that of a league-average passer.

Thinking of fantasy football as a stock market, I've long questioned whether players with well-known weaknesses, such as receivers without competent quarterbacks, actually drop too much in preseason rankings. In the same way it's often smart to bet the under in Saints-Patriots games despite the fact that they're going to put a ton of points on the board, perhaps the wisdom of the fantasy football crowds unnecessarily deflates the value of players with question marks; that is, maybe we're all overvaluing the importance of an elite quarterback, at least in regards to wide receiver fantasy value.

To figure this out, I researched every quarterback with a passer rating of at least 92.0 (elite) and every one with a passer rating below 85.0 (poor) from 2007 to 2011. Then, I looked up the ADP of their top receiver in the following season. Tom Brady turned in a league-best 111.0 passer rating in 2010, for example. His top receiver, Wes Welker, was drafted 15th among wide receivers in 2011 but finished third in standard scoring leagues. I chose to compare the passer rating of a quarterback in Year X to the ADP and final fantasy rank of his top receiver in Year X+1 so that the rating wouldn't be influenced by the performance of the receiver (and vice versa).

At first glance, it appeared as though receivers with poor quarterbacks (those who had a passer rating of 85.0 or lower in the previous season) finished higher than those with elite quarterbacks, at least relative to their ADP. The bad-quarterback receivers dropped an average of eight spots in the rankings as compared to their preseason ADP, while the elite-quarterback receivers actually drop an average of 10 spots in comparison to their ADP. (Note: The majority of receivers didn't live up to their ADP because, as No. 1 options on their respective teams, their ADP didn't allow much room for improvement. The No. 1 overall receiver can't possibly improve upon his ranking, for example).

Actually, 36.7 percent of the receivers in the "bad quarterback" group were able to exceed their preseason ADP, compared to just 16.7 percent for the wide outs in the "elite quarterback" group. So obviously wide receivers with sub-par quarterbacks have been undervalued, right?

Not so fast. The problem was that, with an average ADP of 11.8, the "elite quarterback" group had far more room to drop than the "bad quarterback" group, whose average ADP was way down at 22.8.

To correct for differences in ADP, I assessed only those receivers who were considered WR2 options prior to the season, i.e. those with an ADP between 13 and 24. After doing that, the results changed drastically. Of those receivers with poor quarterbacks in the previous season, only 23.1 percent were able to exceed their ADP. In comparison, 40 percent of the receivers with elite quarterbacks in the prior year were able to exceed their ADP.

Ultimately, I'm not sure there's enough evidence to specifically target or avoid specific receivers based on their quarterback situation. One thing I'll say is that it appears as though the area in which you're drafting might dictate your strategy a bit. The receivers taken early in drafts are highly scrutinized; everyone who drafted Larry Fitzgerald as the No. 2 wide receiver this year was fully aware of his horrible quarterback situation. Since that was certainly a factor in his ADP, it means that Fitzgerald ironically may have possessed some upside with a sub-par quarterback; with everyone already anticipating poor quarterback play, there was room for Fitzgerald to improve upon his ADP if Kevin Kolb had been able to surprise some people (it turns out that he did, but not in a good way).

On the other hand, targeting receivers with elite quarterbacks might be smart in the middle and late rounds. Those types of receivers won't get the targets necessary to make up for poor quarterback play, so they need a Drew Brees-esque player to vault them into relevant fantasy territory. We saw this happen with Greg Jennings in 2008; ranked 19th in the preseason, the remarkable play of Aaron Rodgers was the impetus for Jennings' fourth-place fantasy finish.

- ### The Bottom Line

It's obviously preferable to have wide receivers with elite quarterbacks, but don't forget that the presence of a great quarterback is already factored into the cost of the receiver when you draft him, meaning you can't really gain any advantage from it. There's not much evidence that receivers with poor quarterbacks drop too far in the rankings; in all likelihood, they're probably priced correctly.

However, you could potentially acquire value by drafting receivers with poor quarterbacks in the early part of your draft. Since their quarterback is already a factor in their ADP, better-than-expected quarterback play could catapult their production. Meanwhile, you should probably look at receivers with elite quarterbacks later in the draft. Their upside comes from playing in a high-upside offense, i.e. the quarterback alone can provide the receiver with value.

4 Does week-to-week consistency really exist?

Prior to the 2012 season, I had Minnesota Vikings wide receiver Percy Harvin ranked as my No. 4 overall wide receiver in PPR leagues. In addition to his game-breaking ability, one of the main reasons I ranked Harvin so high is that I consider him "slump-proof." The nature of Harvin's game is so versatile that defenses have a difficult time containing him; he can play outside, in the slot, at running back, or anywhere else you can imagine, catching screens or deep passes and running end-arounds or read-options.

The truth is that Harvin is one of a limited number of players that I consider to possess true week-to-week consistency. The majority of what we perceive as weekly consistency is simply an illusion based on a limited sample size of games.

While certain players possess more season-to-season consistency than others, the short NFL season makes over-analysis of each game unavoidable. When a baseball player goes 1-for-10 over a two-game period, we often chalk it up to being unlucky. Meanwhile, when a quarterback turns in two poor performances in a row, the sky begins to fall in fantasy land.

Imagine cutting up the MLB season into 16-game segments. Each player would have a few segments of really poor play and a few periods of outstanding play. Over the course of the entire 162-game season, those peaks and valleys tend to even out, which is why baseball players have such consistent stats from year to year.

Well, the NFL season is too short for those tendencies to always even out. Thus, we often place more emphasis on individual games than we should because, well, it's all we have to analyze. We label Player X as 'consistent' and Player Y as 'injury-prone,' not realizing we're really just looking at the equivalent of one of those little 16-game slivers that MLB players participate in 10 of each season.

Imagine that a group of 25 receivers all have a 50 percent chance of putting up respectable fantasy numbers in a given game (how you define 'respectable' is irrelevant to this example). For each player, the odds of posting quality fantasy stats are no better or no worse than a coin flip. What kind of results would we expect?

Typically, you'd see around half of players post between seven and nine respectable games. Almost all of the remaining players would fall between four and 12 respectable games, with a few outliers having either an outstanding season of 13-plus big-time performances or a horrible season of three or fewer quality games.

Actually, the results would closely resemble the graph below, which is a series of 400 coin flips I just completed (which sadly takes more time than you'd think and probably says more about me than anything you'll read hereafter). I broke the coin flips down into sets of 16 (to represent each game in an NFL season), tracking the number of heads that came up during each trial of 16 flips.

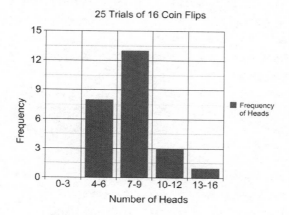

You can see that just over half of the trials ended up with exactly seven, eight, or nine heads. That's to be expected. What many people don't anticipate are the trials that end up as outliers: just a couple or all but a few flips being heads.

Actually, on my first 16 flips, 14 of them were heads. Even knowing that the chances of heads coming up were (almost) 50 percent, I began to think I was a biased coin-flipper. As I continued to flip, however, the number of tails "caught up", i.e. regressed toward the mean, and all was well in the world of randomness.

The takeaway here is that, in any set of random (or near-random) data, we'll see lots of "abnormal" results. If you assign Calvin Johnson a 50 percent chance of going for 100 yards and a touchdown in any given game, he'll probably wind up with somewhere around eight games with such numbers. But there's also a solid chance that he'll appear to have either an unusually outstanding or a very poor year. With a 50 percent chance of 100 yards and a score in any game, Megatron is probably around as likely to have *either* five or 12 stellar games as he is to have exactly eight.

Because the number of games in an NFL season is so low, it's really easy to see patterns in data that aren't really there. Over the course of even a few NFL seasons, we'd expect some players to appear to have a huge degree of weekly consistency, even if consistency were completely random. Similarly, even with total randomness, a handful of players would appear to be "all-or-nothing" fantasy options without much consistency, when in reality they possess just as much consistency as the most reliable performers.

- ## Receivers

To track past rates of consistency for receivers, I looked at high-performing wide receivers over the past two seasons. Of receivers with more than 60 catches, I examined the top 25 and the bottom 25 in terms of yards-per-reception. My hypothesis was that, if weekly consistency exists and is fairly strong, we'd see players with low yards-per-catch totals have the most consistent play. Those players—think Wes Welker, Danny Amendola, Percy Harvin— typically have a much higher reception rate (and often times more targets) than the big-play threats like DeSean Jackson, Mike Wallace, and Brandon Lloyd.

The fact is that the big-play receivers were actually slightly more likely to have consistent play than the low-YPC receivers. That's after I adjusted for stat totals (the top 25 in YPC averaged 1,189 yards and 8.96 TDs per season, compared to 942 yards and 5.12 TDs for the bottom 25 in YPC). On average, the big-play receivers posted games with at least 6.0 percent of their final yardage total just over 9.5 times per year. For the low-YPC players—the ones who many consider to be very consistent on a week-to-week basis—the number was just under 9.5. The results are close enough to conclude that weekly receiving consistency, at least in terms of YPC, doesn't exist.

Like I said, I think there are a handful of players who are truly consistent. Slot receivers in particular (the Harvin's and Cruz's of the world) are more difficult to double-team than X or Z receivers, and thus less likely to be held down in any particular game.

As a general rule of thumb, though, beware of claims that Player X is a "safe bet this week" or Player Y is "really inconsistent." It's really, really easy to find patterns in past data, but really, really difficult to use those patterns to predict future data. As philosophy majors (all 20 of us) like to say, labeling a player as 'consistent' is often done 'ex post facto,' or after the fact. In reality, weekly performances are a whole lot more random, and thus difficult to predict, than you might think.

- **Running Backs**

Even if consistency is valuable, it's quite unpredictable in regards to wide receivers. Among running backs, however, that might not be the case.

Going into this study, my hypothesis was that running backs who catch passes might be more consistent on a weekly basis than non-pass-catching backs because they have more ways to beat defenses. Like Percy Harvin—one of the few receivers I deem as possessing weekly consistency—

running backs who can contribute as receivers necessarily have a lesser degree of volatility because they can score points in two ways.

To take a look at my hypothesis, I sorted all running backs with at least 750 rushing yards over the past two years by the number of receptions they recorded. The top 25 running backs in terms of catches turned in an average of 10.3 "quality starts" per season. I defined a "quality start" as posting at least 6.0 percent of their year-end yardage total in any given game (and thus controlling for differences in talent and system). The pass-catching backs in this group included just who you'd imagine—Arian Foster, Ray Rice, and so on.

On the other hand, the bottom backs in terms of receptions—think Michael Turner, DeAngelo Williams, and Cedric Benson—recorded an average of only 9.0 "quality starts" per season. Remember, backs needed to turn in just 6.0 percent of *their own* year-end yardage total to obtain a "quality start," so the total production from each running back was irrelevant.

Thus, even in non-PPR leagues, I think you need to at least consider drafting pass-catching backs over comparable players who don't haul in many passes. That might seem obvious, but I think the idea stands even if you have players projected for the same number of points. For example, suppose you're deciding between the following two players:

- **Player X: Projected 750 rushing yards, 75 receptions, 600 receiving yards, 4 total touchdowns**
- **Player Y: Projected 1,000 rushing yards, 8 receptions, 50 receiving yards, 9 total touchdowns**

Both players are projected for 155 points in non-PPR formats, but Player X is probably the superior option. Even without the same red zone prowess and what is likely fewer carries, he'll probably be more consistent than Player Y on a week-to-week basis. This makes him less volatile, and thus probably more worthy of your selection.

During the season, this information might be valuable for close calls regarding who to start in a given week. If you're the favorite in your matchup and you're deciding between players similar to Player X and Player Y, the former is the better option because he's safer. As the favorite, you want to minimize risk. If you're the underdog, however, you might actually want to consider Player Y (in non-PPR leagues only, of course). With play that is inherently more volatile, you'll need that upside as the underdog to win your matchup.

- **Quarterbacks**

To determine if any certain quarterbacks are more consistent than others, I studied all quarterbacks who have thrown for at least 3,000 yards in a single season since 2007. Then, I sorted those passers by rushing yards.

If I'm correct in my hypothesis that versatile quarterbacks are consistent on a week-to-week basis, we'd expect rushing quarterbacks to have more "quality starts" than the non-rushing quarterbacks. It turns out I was wrong. The top 25 quarterbacks in terms of single-season rushing yards posted an average of 10.1 games with at least 6.0 percent of their total fantasy points. Meanwhile, the pocket passers averaged 10.8 games with at least 6.0 percent of their year-end fantasy points.

So why haven't the rushing quarterbacks—a list that includes Cam Newton and Aaron Rodgers—been more consistent than the static quarterbacks? My hunch is that, despite some big names in the mobile quarterback category, the majority of the pocket passers are simply better than the running quarterbacks. In the latter category, for example, I examined five seasons from Peyton Manning alone. Drew Brees, Kurt Warner, and Brett Favre also fell into the non-rushing quarterback category on more than one occasion. On the other hand, some of the big rushing quarterbacks over the past five seasons include David Garrard, Josh Freeman, Ryan Fitzpatrick, and Matt Cassel.

Thus, I think what we're seeing is that there really aren't all that many passers whose rushing prowess can really make a fantasy impact. Actually, only Cam Newton and Michael Vick (twice) have thrown for 3,000 yards and rushed for over 400 yards in the past five seasons. Only one more quarterback—Tim Tebow—has rushed for more than 400 yards, regardless of passing yardage. Of the three combined 3,000/400 seasons from Newton and Vick, the average number of quality starts was 11.7.

Ultimately, I think rushing quarterbacks really do possess more weekly consistency than other passers. The problem is that there aren't many true dual-threat quarterbacks out there. Sorry, but comparing a mobile quarterback like Jason Campbell or Ryan Fitzpatrick to Cam Newton is ridiculous.

As the nature of the college game changes and more RGIII-esque quarterbacks enter the league, you'll see a real change in how quarterbacks are viewed in fantasy circles. Why bank on Tom Brady beating defenses through the air when you can bet on Newton scoring points with both his arm and legs? Newton, RGIII, and future NFL quarterbacks can throw for only 150 yards and still post spectacular fantasy numbers. While the risk of injury is always slightly greater with rushing quarterbacks, the season-to-season and even week-to-week consistency is probably great enough make up for that risk.

- ## The Bottom Line

Prior to the season, your primary concern should be the consistency of each player on a year-to-year basis—a topic I'll analyze shortly. The truth is that most of what we view as weekly consistency is an illusion, and even the consistency that exists is extremely difficult to predict.

However, there's probably at least a moderate amount of consistency for pass-catching running backs. Even in leagues that don't reward points for receptions, running backs who catch passes are more "slump-proof" than those who don't. In general, you should target players who can do a lot of things well to help you win games, whether it's rushing for receivers like Harvin, catching passes for running backs, or running for *true* dual-threat quarterbacks.

Understanding consistency can also help you make in-season moves. If you're debating between starting two players, side with the versatility.

5 How does the consistency of certain positions affect a draft board?

If you knew without any doubt that one kicker would (hypothetically) score 1,000 points this season, you'd do everything in your power to secure him, right? Even if you were limited to drafting just a single kicker, you might do so in the first round and hope he's the lucky one to outscore all other kickers by about 800 points. If you get it right, the fantasy crown is yours.

In the same league, one shrewd owner waits until the last round to draft his kicker. Even with 1,000 fantasy points on the line, he stocks up on skill positions as per usual. Does he know something the rest of his league mates don't?

The fact is that the majority of fantasy owners either ignore or don't fully comprehend position volatility, and it can have dire consequences on their draft strategy. If a particular position had zero predictability—meaning it was impossible to accurately project—we should completely ignore it.

In reality, the kicker position has zero consistency from year to year. As a whole, the position is impossible to predict; pick a starting kicker on any team you'd like, and he'll be just about as likely to lead the league in fantasy points as any other kicker.

In other words, the kicker position has amazingly high volatility.

Smart fantasy owners thrive on making accurate predictions. After all, that's really what the draft is about—making predictions that are more accurate than the general consensus in an effort to acquire value with each pick. Without consistency, however, predictions are useless.

That's why understanding the consistency of each position as a whole is vital to garnering maximum value on draft day. All other things being equal, you want the players whose 2012 play is most likely to match up with your projections. The greater the positional and individual consistency, the more likely that is to happen.

So when you're deciding between A.J. Green and Aaron Rodgers with the ninth overall pick this season, keep some of this information in mind. One of those players, in all likelihood, is supremely superior to the other in your league; do you know which one is the "right" choice?

- ## The Big Picture
There's no doubt that each of your fantasy draft picks should be taken on a case-by-case basis, but position-wide trends should certainly influence your decisions. Specifically, understanding the

consistency of each position as a whole can help you create an accurate draft board.

When I wrote the first *Fantasy Football for Smart People* book I calculated the year-to-year consistency of each position to help owners acquire a solid understanding of just how easy it is to project points for each player.

Those consistency correlations can also be thought of as confidence ratings—that is, how confident can you be that your projection for a player is spot on? If the strength of correlation for quarterback fantasy points were theoretically 1.00, we'd be able to accurately project each player's points each and every time. If the correlation were 0.0, as is the case with kickers, projections would be useless—picking a player with a season-to-season consistency correlation of zero is synonymous to playing roulette. There's no way to beat the house.

Luckily for us, accurate projections are attainable. The degree to which we can predict the play of specific players, however, varies based on a multitude of factors, their position being perhaps the most important of those. So without further ado, here are my findings. . .

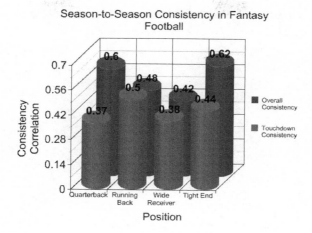

Above, you can see the consistency of each position from one season to the next. This data was taken over the past decade.

For all intents and purposes, you can think of each correlation as the percentage of a player's stats that carry over from one year to the next. For example, you can see the overall consistency correlation for quarterback points is 0.60. This means, on average, 60 percent of a quarterback's points from the previous season are repeated in the current year, while 40 percent regress toward a league mean. If Player X scored 400 points but the league mean for quarterbacks was 250, a solid baseline projection for that player would be 400(0.6) + 250 (0.4), or 340 points.

One of the beneficial products of utilizing such correlations into projections is a natural implementation of regression toward the mean. If a player scored 400 fantasy points, for example, chances are he overachieved and is thus likely to post fewer fantasy points the following season. A formula that uses consistency correlations automatically factors regression toward the mean into account, and is thus inherently more accurate than a simple mirroring of prior stats.

Another benefit of utilizing consistency is that it provides a measurement of confidence. We can project stats all day, but it means nothing if we can't assign a likelihood of occurrence. Knowing that 60 percent of a quarterback's stats or 38 percent of a wide receiver's touchdowns will repeat themselves from one season to the next is useful information that can and should influence your rankings. Going back to our 1,000-point kicker example, it doesn't matter how many points you project a player to score (or even the gap between him and the next player at his position) if you can't be confident in your prediction.

- **Breaking Down the Positions**

Looking at the overall consistency correlations for each of the four skill positions, there are some interesting numbers. You might be surprised to see that tight end is actually the most consistent (and thus predictable) position in fantasy football, followed closely by quarterback, then running back, and finally wide receiver. Actually, only 42 percent of a typical wide receiver's performance carries over from year to year.

Interestingly, the distribution of preseason projections matches up with the above graph quite well. Using a simple regression of players' stats, I calculated the difference in players' preseason ranks and their final finish. The graph displays this movement for quarterbacks, running backs, and tight ends.

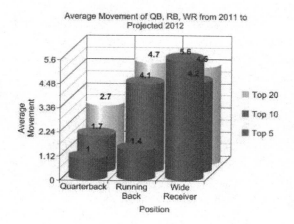

It is worth noting that I didn't use any subjective analysis in creating the projections for this analysis; I simply used a regression of efficiency stats (such as yards-per-reception, yards-per-carry, and so on), then calculated the projected points.

You can see that the wide receiver position is dramatically more volatile than running back and quarterback, particularly early in the draft. Among the top five quarterbacks from any given season, the projected change in rank is just one spot per player. This means that Aaron Rodgers, Drew Brees, and the other top-tier quarterbacks are highly unlikely to fall out of the top five, barring injury.

Interestingly, the top-tier running backs are nearly just as consistent. Despite an overall consistency correlation of just 0.48 (compared to 0.60 for quarterbacks), the top five running backs are projected to move an average of only 1.4 spots from one year to the next. Acquiring one of these top-tier players is wholly important if you own an early pick this season.

On the other hand, top five receivers typically move an average of 5.6 spots from one year to the next. That means a guy like Calvin Johnson is probably more likely to end up seventh in wide receiver points than first. If that seems impossible, go ahead and look at the final wide receiver rankings from the past few seasons—rarely will you see the same players again and again. Meanwhile, you can draft Aaron Rodgers or Arian Foster and take their 2012 fantasy points straight to the bank.

Outside of the top tier, you can see the volatility at the running back position skyrockets. Meanwhile, the lack of volatility of middle-tier receivers is really amazing; the No. 20-ranked receiver in the preseason usually moves fewer spots than the No. 5-ranked receiver.

Similarly, top 10 wide receivers are nearly just as consistent as top 10 running backs, meaning the third, fourth, and fifth rounds are a great time to target receivers. If you were able to nab a top-tier running back in the first round and the best non-receiver in the second, you'd be in a great position to stock up on elite or near-elite receiver talent in the middle rounds.

- **Practical Application**

The purpose of implementing consistency into your rankings isn't to scare you away from taking any receiver in the first few rounds of the draft, but rather to provide an understanding of which positions tend to remain stable from year to year. If you're deciding between a tight end and a wide receiver in the third round and everything else seems equal, you might want to go with the player whose performance is most likely to repeat itself.

I think the consistency correlations are most useful at the top of the draft. In the first round or two, your goal should be to minimize downside. In that area, everyone's upside is high. Actually, the top-ranked players are really the "outliers" from the previous season; they overachieved and their production is probably going to decline in the subsequent season. Thus, the best you can hope for is really a repeat performance, which would mean you really just got what you paid for.

If you have the first overall pick, for example, chances are your selection won't live up to his draft spot. The cost is so great that your pick can only provide a marginal return on investment. That means you should maximize the floor of your early picks; that is, select safe players whose play isn't volatile. Safe picks in the early rounds are boring, but they win fantasy championships. The middle and late rounds are the times to take your risks.

- **The Bottom Line**

The consistency correlations I outlined can be extremely useful, so there are a number of take-home points for this section:

1. Projections are useless without consistency. It doesn't matter how many points you project a player to score if his performance is inherently volatile.

2. Tight end is the most consistent position in fantasy football, followed by quarterback, running back, and wide receiver.

3. Yards are typically easier to predict than touchdowns, especially for quarterbacks and tight ends.

4. At the top of the draft, you should emphasize safety. That means you should focus on drafting consistent play instead of upside.

4. Elite running backs are nearly as consistent as the top quarterbacks. The NFL's best running backs are both consistent and scarce, making them extremely valuable.

5. Meanwhile, top-tier receivers aren't nearly as consistent as the other skill positions. If you're going to draft a receiver in the first two rounds, you better make sure he's displayed that he can continually rank among the league's elite.

6. You shouldn't target or avoid a specific position entirely because of consistency, but the correlations I provided can be a framework for your drafting. If you're deciding between two players at different positions, it's generally better to go with the most consistent position in the early rounds (when you want to minimize risk) and the more volatile position in the middle and late rounds (when you're seeking upside).

6 How do you really find value in fantasy football drafts?

Every summer, I get a lot of questions from fantasy owners regarding the value of certain players. Would you draft Player X, and is Player Y a good value? Even though I obviously like some players more than others, my answer is always the same: it depends.

- **The NFL and Fantasy Football Value**

In April 2012, the Philadelphia Eagles traded cornerback Asante Samuel to the Atlanta Falcons for just a seventh-round selection. Samuel is past his prime, but he was certainly still a starting-caliber defensive back at the time of the trade. Samuel yielded just a 52.4 passer rating in 2011 (fifth-best in the NFL), and Pro Football Focus graded him as the league's 12th best player at the position.

If the NFL invoked an economic structure similar to that of Major League Baseball, Samuel would have fetched far more than a late-round draft pick. In a league without a salary cap, the cost of players extends only as far as the owner's checkbook. Many of baseball's billionaire owners don't mind overspending in order to secure elite players. If money is no object, the value of baseball players relates only to their ability to play well.

In the NFL, however, teams are limited by a strict enforcement of a salary cap. The cost of signing players is greater due to the actual contract, its hindrance on a team's salary cap management, and the inability of an organization to sign other players. All of these aspects make up what is known as the opportunity cost of having a player on your team.

As it relates to Samuel, the Eagles owed him $21.3 million over the next two years of his deal. Even though Samuel was a good cornerback, his performance and age probably didn't warrant that kind of money. Assuming owner Jeffrey Lurie wouldn't have minded shelling out $21.3 million to Samuel from a financial standpoint, the figure would still have been a major blow to Philly's salary cap, blocking their ability to sign other players. Despite being a quality player, Samuel wasn't of particularly great value to the Eagles.

- **Finding Value in Fantasy Drafts**

For fantasy owners, the round in which a player is selected represents his "contract." Thus, a single player can possess both great and horrible value depending where he gets drafted, with the opportunity cost being the loss of the pick. Later rounds represent a lower opportunity cost.

We know a player's value in the NFL and fantasy football isn't based solely on his projected performance, but also the opportunity cost of acquiring him. A vital aspect of that idea is that different players can hold various amounts of value for different teams.

Let's go back to Samuel. His contract was the primary reason the Eagles were willing to let him walk, but another important factor was the Eagles' roster. With Nnamdi Asomugha and Dominique Rodgers-Cromartie also at cornerback, Samuel's potential value to the team was minimal at his $21.3 million price tag.

Just as a player's fantasy value is determined largely by his draft spot, it also can fluctuate depending on which owner selects him. Let's head to the third round of your upcoming fantasy draft. You've managed to land Ray Rice and Maurice Jones-Drew in the first two rounds, and Matt Forte has somehow fallen to your pick in the third.

For most owners, Forte would represent incredible value. For you, not so much. The opportunity cost of selecting Forte is monumental, as you would be forced to again bypass the selection of other positions. Forte's projected points might be substantial, but the points he'll be projected to score for *your* squad would be minimal. *Note: I'll be discussing the value of a RB-RB-RB draft strategy later in the book.

While players clearly don't have a totally objective value, they do possess a semi-objective value as it relates to your team (based on your rankings). To forgo the selection of a "need" position, the player you draft must possess great semi-objective value. Thus, "value" picks aren't as straightforward as they seem; the value of a selection isn't based only on what you acquire, but also what you *don't*.

That last sentence is an important one, as it highlights the primary vindication of the value-based draft strategy I've advocated in the past. Any worthwhile draft strategy must possess an overarching vision; draft strategies like "Best Player Available" are too shortsighted, necessarily limiting the projected points you can acquire down the road in favor of more now.

Projecting future picks is not only an important component of understanding opportunity cost, but also an intrinsic one. The cost of drafting any particular player, then, comes not only with the loss of a pick, but also in the *inability to select other players*, both at the current selection and future ones.

- **Minimizing "Lost" Points**

You may have noticed a different type of mindset developing here. Whereas most fantasy owners are concerned about acquiring the most possible projected points with each pick, your focus should be "losing" the least. If the perfect fantasy team represents the acquisition of the most possible total projected points, your job is to minimize the loss of projected points at each selection, and that minimization requires forward-thinking the more shortsighted BPA strategy does not.

A fantasy football draft is really no different than the stock market. Both stock traders and fantasy owners seek to leverage knowledge into value acquisition, and that value is the result of cost minimization. And just as game theory is a useful tool in the fantasy owner's arsenal, a fundamental understanding of public perception is vital to traders.

Stocks are not inherently good or bad. Rather, those designations come in relation to the price of the stock. The merits of purchasing Microsoft stock, for example, cannot be determined without knowledge of the share price. Likewise, players are not valuable to fantasy owners outside of a proper understanding of their opportunity cost.

The goal of investors is to sell stocks at their peak and buy them at their lowest point. When a stock is at its highest price, the number is likely not representative of the stock's true worth. In most cases, stocks tend to fall after they reach an all-time high due to regression toward the mean.

Similarly, fantasy owners are in the business of "buying" players whose perceived value is lower than their actual value, and "selling" players whose perceived value *exceeds* their actual value. Such a "buy low, sell high" mentality is fundamental to both stock trading and fantasy drafting.

- **Understanding Public Perception**

At the heart of the value determination process for both traders and fantasy owners is a keen knowledge of public perception. Traders seek to predict which stocks will become popular among the public prior to that stock's share price rising. Similarly, fantasy owners must recognize which players have too low of a price tag (or Average Draft Position).

Both share price and ADP are set by the public. Traders and fantasy owners must understand how the public perceives stocks and football players to enhance value. For the latter group, the worth comes in not knowing which players to draft, but more importantly, *when* to draft them. Remember, neither stocks nor players have inherent value; value is a reflection of both actual worth and opportunity cost, the latter trait being influenced heavily by public perception.

- **The Bottom Line**

If there's one thing to understand when drafting players, it's that their value is inherently tied to that draft position. It's not enough to get the players you want; you need to get the players you want at the right spots. If you pay a third-round pick for a player you could have drafted in the fifth round, you made a mistake, regardless of how well the player performs in the upcoming season. Don't ever forget that the cost of a player includes the players you *can't* select if you draft him.

7 What's the typical age (and rate) of decline for each position?

Did you know running backs come into the NFL at near peak efficiency? How about that quarterbacks can produce elite fantasy numbers well into their 30s? Did you know the peak age of production for wide receivers is 26? Up until a little while ago, neither did I.

Understanding the age at which players break down has numerous uses in both redraft and keeper leagues. Actually, I'd argue that drafting with a keen understanding of rates of decline is one of the easiest ways to improve your team. It's also something hardly anyone does.

The ultimate goal with every single one of your fantasy football picks is to acquire players whose past production doesn't reflect how they'll perform in the future. There's no better way to predict when a player will break out than to know at which ages other players at his position have done it in the past.

- **Running Backs**

Heading into the 2012 season, many fantasy owners were high on Benjarvus Green-Ellis. After proving to be a touchdown machine in New England, "The Lawfirm" was set to rack up touches as Cincinnati's lead running back.

Green-Ellis did indeed see a heavy workload in 2012 with 300 total touches. Despite finishing with the 10th-most touches for any running back in the league, Green-Ellis checked in at just 22nd in fantasy points at the position, due primarily to horrible efficiency; 3.9 YPC, 4.7 YPR, and a touchdown on just two percent of his touches.

So what went wrong? Green-Ellis was in a running back-friendly situation in Cincinnati. Further, at age 27, Green-Ellis was just entering the prime of his career, right? Maybe not.

I recently researched the production for all running backs with at least 100 touches in a season since 2000. I charted those backs based on their total production and efficiency at each age.

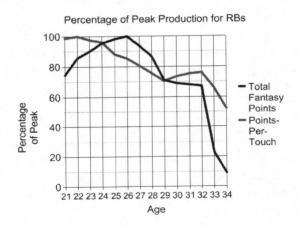

Percentage of Peak Production for RBs

Contrary to popular belief, running backs don't see a dramatic drop in their total production around age 30. Instead, that decline typically occurs after their age 26 season. Yes, the typical running back's overall production peaks before his 27th birthday. From there, the drop is a steep one, with the average 29-year old back producing only 70 percent of the fantasy points he generated at his peak.

The decline in efficiency is even more amazing. The average NFL running back records the highest points-per-touch at age 22—usually his rookie season or second year in the league. From there, the drop is pretty steady until age 30, when there's a slight increase. That small jump is probably due to more talented backs staying in the league while lesser players have been forced out. The rise is short-lived, with the average running back seeing a dramatic decrease in efficiency by age 33.

Looking at the chart, it's pretty clear that running backs don't peak at age 30. Actually, if you're considering drafting a 30-year old back, you can probably expect his production to remain steady for at least a couple of years. That production is nowhere near his past peak, but as long as that's factored into your decision on where to draft him, you should be fine.

The running backs that you might want to avoid most are those around the ages of 27 to 29. Most backs in that range are going to see a drop in production and efficiency—often a dramatic one—but it usually won't be accounted for in their ADP. That means you'll be paying for a player as if he's producing at his peak when he's more likely to give you about 85 percent of what you're expecting.

The best value on running backs, perhaps, is in the 21-24 range. Young running backs who have produced at a good-but-not-great level are typically undervalued. By age 24, both their efficiency and overall production should be within about five percent of its peak.

Looking at the graph, you can see just how valuable rookie and second-year running backs can be in dynasty leagues. Those players will inevitably see spikes in production, whereas runners in their mid-to-late 20s will likely see a drop in the coming years.

Let's assume you're considering two backs: a 23-year old coming off of a season with 1,000 total yards and eight touchdowns and a 27-year old back coming off of a season with 1,200 yards and 11 touchdowns. For most, the decision to grab the older runner would be an easy one. But let's take a look at their three-year outlooks, assuming they follow the typical running back production curve. . .

23-Year Old Back (Year Y = 148 points)

- **Year Y+1 = 155 points**

- **Year Y+2 = 167 points**
- **Year Y+3 = 170 points**

Three-Year Average: 164 points

27-Year Old Back (Year Y = 186 points)

- **Year Y+1 = 179 points**
- **Year Y+2 = 163 points**
- **Year Y+3 = 130 points**

Three-Year Average: 157 points

Although the older back would be projected to score more points in the upcoming season, he'd be below the younger back in the subsequent two years. Over a three-year period—a good timeframe to consider in dynasty leagues—the younger back with the lesser stats would be projected at an average of seven fewer points per season. Those are points you'd miss if you believed running backs were in their peak years until age 30.

It's also interesting to see just how little deviation there is in the projections for the young running back as opposed to the 27-year old—a difference of only 15 points compared to 49. That's pretty good evidence that young running backs are probably safer bets than older ones. Whereas it can be tempting to hang your hat on an old, "reliable" back like Steven Jackson, it's the running backs ages 23 to 26 who are really the safe picks. In the early portions of the draft when your goal should be risk-minimization, you might be able to find value—and safety—in young running backs.

It's important to note that the graph is hardly a comprehensive draft tool; there are tons of factors that go into each player's stock, so it shouldn't be used in isolation. However, it's still useful to know that running backs typically peak far earlier than most people believe, and you can utilize that information to your advantage.

And when other owners are jumping on the prototypical steady 28-year old running back because he's still on "the right side of 30," you can acquire value on the young guns who aren't on the wrong side of 26.

- **Quarterbacks**

Heading into the 2013 season, there are a handful of big-name quarterbacks nearing the tail end of their careers; Drew Brees (34), Tom Brady (36), and Peyton Manning (37) are still playing at a high level, but how long can they maintain it? Maybe longer than you think.

While running backs are an "anti-wine"—getting worse with age—quarterbacks are much different. I charted the production for starting quarterbacks over the past two decades.

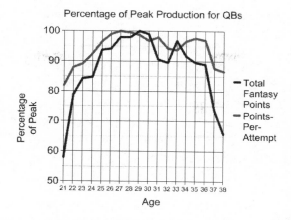

Percentage of Peak Production for QBs

Unlike running backs, quarterbacks typically increase their overall production and efficiency at a gradual pace. Quarterback efficiency peaks at age 27 and overall fantasy production peaks two years later. Remarkably, quarterbacks have maintained their high levels of efficiency until their mid-30s. Meanwhile, overall production has dipped at two points—around age 31 and again at age 37.

Interestingly, there's a small jump in both efficiency and production for quarterbacks in their mid- to late-30s. That's likely due to a "survivor bias"—the fact that the best quarterbacks remain in the league and continue to play at a high level while the lesser passers have been forced out. That explains the jump in total fantasy points per quarterback at age 33; quarterbacks don't really get better at that age, but rather the elite ones—Brett Favre, Tom Brady, and so on—remain in the league and boost the numbers.

- **Using the Chart in 2013 and Beyond**

Understanding historic trends in quarterback decline can be useful in both redraft and keeper leagues. While other owners are perhaps downgrading Brady this year in favor of a player like Cam Newton, you can rest easy knowing that Brady's overall production is likely to resemble that from 2012.

In keeper leagues, you can and should take advantage of the value of middle-aged quarterbacks. In terms of overall production, quarterbacks typically post around 90 percent of their peak (or greater) from ages 25 to 36. That's a huge window, meaning jumping on a 31-year old quarterback coming off of a lackluster season might not be such a bad idea.

In studying quarterbacks, it was evident that they age in a much different manner than running backs. The ages of decline are obviously different, but so are the rates. Running backs typically see a gradual decline; the production for a 32-year old running back is often slightly worse than it was the prior year, which was slightly worse than it was before that, and so on.

On the other hand, quarterbacks generally "lose it" all at once. Instead of seeing Brees, Brady, & Co. progressively produce worse numbers, we'll probably see a more distinct drop before they eventually leave the league. That can make it more difficult to project quarterbacks because it's really an "all-or-nothing" situation.

Thus, instead of projecting a player like Peyton Manning with, say, 90 percent of his 2012 fantasy points, it's really more of a game of percentages. Since quarterback production typically falls off of a cliff, we're better off saying that Manning has a good chance to repeat his 2012 production, but there's a relatively small chance that 2013 is the year he tanks. As he continues to age, the probability increases. That means aging quarterbacks can potentially offer value if you're willing to take on that risk in favor of their upside. Manning in particular is perhaps a risk because of his age and health, but there's still a really good chance that he finishes 2013 as a top five quarterback.

- ## The "Real" Quarterback Prime Years

The chart displays historic data for quarterbacks, but there might be some reason to believe that the range of peak years for current quarterbacks has been extended. First, as I showed earlier, rookie quarterbacks have produced at unbelievable rates over the past few seasons. They might be outliers, but quarterbacks are coming into the league more prepared than ever before. Plus, with NFL teams finally altering their offenses to fit the skill sets of their rookie passers (see Cam Newton and RGIII), first and second-year quarterbacks can really produce.

On the other end of the spectrum, aging quarterbacks have been able to produce at unprecedented levels. With advances in conditioning and injury prevention, there's good reason to think that "40 is the new 37" when it comes to quarterbacks. If that's the case, you can add Manning (37) to the list of "over-the-hill" quarterbacks worthy of consideration in 2013 redraft leagues.

- **Wide Receivers**

After a 2011 season in which he participated in only seven games and tied his career-low for touchdowns, Texans wide receiver Andre Johnson exploded for 112 receptions and 1,598 yards in 2012. The breakout wasn't really too surprising for one of the game's elite receivers; Johnson had three prior 100-catch seasons and two years with at least 1,500 yards. We know that Johnson won't be able to continue his dominance forever, but when will his decline strike?

Running backs are on one end of the NFL career spectrum, typically seeing a gradual drop in efficiency almost immediately after they enter the league. On the other end are quarterbacks, who can accomplish great things late in their careers. The outlook for wide receivers probably falls somewhere between the two.

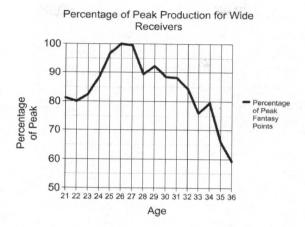

Like quarterbacks, wide receivers take some time to develop. There have been only six rookie wide receivers since 2000 to finish in the top 24 at their position. That's pretty remarkable, especially when you consider that three of them—A.J. Green, Julio Jones, and Torrey Smith—came in a single year.

Unlike quarterbacks, however, wide receivers can't sustain a high level of play into their mid-30s. They're more like running backs in that they typically see a gradual decline once they hit their peak. That peak has historically come at age 26. Actually, the three-year window from ages 25 to 27 is often the most productive for wide receivers. Over the past decade, receivers in each age of that range—25, 26, and 27—have produced over 97 percent of their peak production, as a whole.

If we loosen the parameters of "peak production," you can see that receivers can be quite productive for a fairly long period of time. Historically, they've been at or near 90 percent of their peak production from ages 24 to 31—a period of time much longer than that for running backs, who are at or near 90 percent of peak production from ages 23 to 28.

So what's the age of decline for wide receivers? As usual, there's no single number after which receivers become ineffective, but they usually see a semi-steep drop in production around age 28, and then another around age 33. Actually, if a 27-year old wide receiver who just hauled in 100 receptions for 1,500 yards and 10 touchdowns followed the typical wide receiver career path exactly, he'd post around 90 grabs for 1,350 yards and nine touchdowns in the following season and, by age 33, those numbers would drop to right around 75 catches for 1,125 yards and seven scores. By age 35, most wide receivers are washed up. The few that remain in the league typically have a difficult time putting up respectable fantasy numbers.

- **Using the Wide Receiver Aging Chart**

Going back to Andre Johnson, we know based on historic data that a drop in production is likely. If you're projecting Johnson to duplicate his 2012 numbers in 2013, you'll probably be disappointed. It's not as if Johnson can't do it or that his stats will follow the typical wide receiver aging pattern to a tee, but rather the likelihood of continued dominance decreases each year, especially as he enters his mid-30s.

While we can certainly use historic decline rates in redraft leagues for players like Johnson, the numbers are far more useful for those in keeper or dynasty leagues. If you're looking at two receivers with similar production, but one is coming off of his age 24 season and the other off of his age 27 season, your choice should be clear.

Let's break it down. Suppose both your 24 and 27-year old targets recently recorded 90 catches for 1,400 yards and 10 touchdowns. If you're in a league that allows you to keep players for three years, you might assume there isn't much difference between the two receivers; the 27-year old should be fine until he's 30, right?

Not so fast. If each receiver's future production resembled that of the average wide receiver, their projected numbers over the next three seasons would be quite different:

24-Year Old: 296 catches for 4,605 yards and 32 touchdowns (949 PPR points—316 points per season)

27-Year Old: 246 catches for 3,819 yards and 27 touchdowns (790 PPR points—263 points per season)

Pretty remarkable, huh? The "same" players in terms of overall talent and situation, on average, would be separated by 53 points per year based solely on a three-year gap in age. So if you want to know why you should have A.J. Green ranked ahead of Calvin Johnson in dynasty leagues, this is it.

- **Tight Ends**

Let's get right into it. I charted tight end production over the past decade-plus, sorted by age.

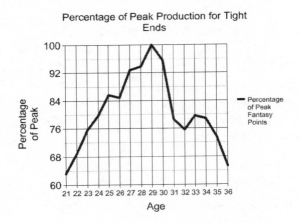

Percentage of Peak Production for Tight Ends

If that graph were a mountain, it would be difficult to climb on both ends. That's because tight ends have historically had a smaller range of peak years than quarterbacks, receivers, and even running backs. Tight ends take a long time to develop—the probability of a rookie tight end posting respectable fantasy numbers is almost zero—and they see a steep decline in their early-30s.

Historically, the typical tight end has produced only four seasons with at least 90 percent of his peak production. In that way, they're very comparable to wide receivers, who also record only a few elite years. The difference is that wide receivers sustain a decent level of play for a much longer time than tight ends.

But why? It's possible that the wear and tear of playing the tight end position takes its toll. By the time tight ends hit their 30s, they're just worn out. That might change with the rise of pure pass-catching tight ends who don't have to deal with the hassle of blocking, but it's unclear right now.

To show you the small window of opportunity for the average tight end, check out the following chart.

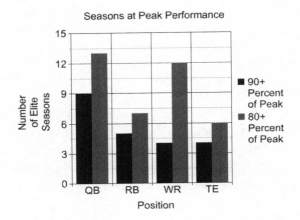

Seasons at Peak Performance

This gives you a really good idea of the number of quality (80+ percent of peak) and elite (90+ percent of peak) seasons for the average player at each position. Unsurprisingly, quarterbacks have the longest windows with an average of 13 quality seasons. Meanwhile, tight ends have the fewest quality seasons (six) and elite seasons (four).

So what does this mean for you in fantasy leagues? I think it actually both helps and hurts tight end value, depending what league you're in. In dynasty leagues, tight ends have to be downgraded since most of them won't provide you with long-term production. In redraft leagues, however, the lack of tight ends playing at an elite level at any given time could actually inflate their value. Remember, a fundamental concept of sound fantasy football drafting strategy is scarcity; elite tight ends are a scare (and surprisingly consistent) resource, meaning they're valuable.

In both dynasty and redraft leagues, target tight ends entering their mid-20s. It's in that range that most tight ends see a dramatic spike in play. It's unclear why it takes tight ends so long to develop in the NFL, but it tends to happen pretty quickly when it does. By targeting mid-20s tight ends before they break out (and passing on middle-aged tight ends prior to their inevitable decline), you can acquire value.

And one last point: Tony Gonzalez is a freak of nature and none of this applies to him. Draft him until he's 55 years old.

- ## The Bottom Line

Age-based projections are the way of the future, but they're rarely utilized. I'd go as far as to say that there aren't more than a couple player traits you should consider before looking at age. The reason is that rates of decline aren't utilized by the majority of fantasy owners, so they're not factored into ADP.

Owners in dynasty leagues in particular need to have a keen grasp on age-based projections. It's extremely useful to know that the difference between a 26 and 28-year old running backs is far different than that for tight ends of the same age.

Running backs enter the league at near peak efficiency, and it's a steady decline from there. Their peak total production typically occurs around age 26. Quarterbacks take longer to develop, but they can sustain a high level of play well into their 30s. Wide receivers also take a relatively long time to develop, although their play usually drops off by the time they hit their late-20s. Nonetheless, the average wide receiver produces a remarkable 12 seasons with at least 80 percent of their peak production. That number is only six for tight ends—the position with the smallest window of opportunity.

8 Should your first three draft picks be three running backs?

In 2012, I participated in a draft for a 10-team league in which I (shockingly, and for the first time in about 50 straight drafts) drew the first overall selection. The league is a thin one—we start two running backs, two receivers, and a flex. Arian Foster was the obvious choice to begin the draft, but as players came off of the board with the subsequent 18 selections, I began to rethink my draft strategy.

Once I was on the clock with the No. 20 and No. 21 overall picks, I was left with an interesting dilemma; choose another running back and a stud wide receiver, such as A.J. Green, or bypass a receiver altogether and draft three straight running backs to begin the draft.

Up until that night, I hadn't drafted three running backs to start a draft since I took Shaun Alexander, Willis McGahee, and Rudi Johnson quite a few years ago. But the lack of depth in this particular league—it was a 10-teamer that required only two starting receivers—got me thinking if it was prudent to load up on backs early. That's exactly the strategy I employed, adding Jamaal Charles and Ryan Mathews to form what I thought was perhaps the top RB-RB-Flex combination of my career. Thanks for ruining it, Ryan!

Anyway, after the draft, I decided to run some numbers to see if I made the right move. Although my draft was shallow, I wanted to know if, with the dearth of top-tier talent at the running back position, securing three of the top 15 or so players at the position is a smart move. In my particular league, I knew that 1) Ryan Mathews would eventually be my every-week flex, and 2) the depth at wide receiver would allow me to obtain quality starters in the fourth and fifth rounds (I landed Dez Bryant and Dwayne Bowe).

To answer my question, I decided to calculate the projected points you could be expected to obtain from both positions—running back and wide receiver—based on your draft slot. For example, using ADP, I determined that drafting three straight running backs and then two receivers in the first five rounds from the No. 1 draft slot would provide you with, on average, this combination of players: RB1-RB12-RB13-WR18-WR19. I repeated that process for three draft combinations and two more draft slots (No. 6 and No. 12).

When calculating total projected points, I simply used my own projections for the 2012 season. While my projections undoubtedly differ from your projections or anyone else's, the range and deviation of projected points is likely very similar for all of us. I had my No. 18 overall wide receiver projected to score 226 points in a PPR format, for example.

Chances are your No. 18 receiver was around that number as well, even if we aren't talking about the same guy. By the way, the No. 18 overall receiver ended up scoring 212 points in PPR leagues.

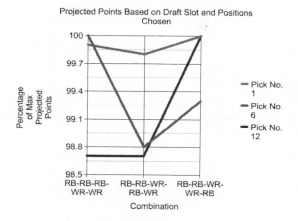

The graph shows the percentage of peak points scored for three position combinations in three different draft slots. Each draft slot has one optimal position combination which is obviously listed at 100 percent. Here are those optimal combinations for the three draft slots:

- **No. 1 Pick: RB-RB-WR-WR-RB**
- **No. 6 Pick: RB-RB-RB-WR-WR**
- **No. 12 Pick: RB-RB-WR-WR-RB**

I was surprised to learn that, for the No. 1 overall draft slot, the combination of picks doesn't really matter. Drafting RB-RB-WR-RB-WR led to just three fewer projected points than RB-RB-WR-WR-RB. Part of the reasoning for that, I think, is that when choosing at the end of a round, you get two straight selections. Thus, placing a running back in the fourth spot or fifth spot doesn't matter—it's still the same player.

The effect is a bit more pronounced for the No. 6 and No. 12 overall selections. The worst possible lineup of the bunch is RB-RB-RB-WR-WR from the last draft slot, which I have projected to score 98.7 percent as many points as RB-RB-WR-WR-RB.

Interestingly, the No. 6 overall pick is the only spot at which drafting three straight running backs leads to peak projected points. I would have thought the No. 1 slot would have also had peak production from a RB-RB-RB combination, although RB-RB-RB from that slot is projected to score 23 more points than RB-RB-RB from the No. 6 slot.

Ultimately, what is most amazing about this little study is the incredible accuracy of the market (ADP). You'd think there might be a few weaknesses among the masses that a shrewd owner could exploit, but I don't think that's the case. At least in regards to running backs and wide receivers in the first five rounds, the incredible similarity of each draft combination suggests the general public has developed a rather accurate depiction of reality.

- ## The Bottom Line

There really isn't too much of a difference between RB-RB-RB and RB-RB-WR. In the first few rounds, you should simply be focused on taking safe, undervalued players. Interestingly, drafting three straight running backs—as long as they represent value—doesn't seem to help or hurt in any major way.

9 What type of player should you draft in the late rounds?

After I wrote *Fantasy Football for Smart People: How to Dominate Your Draft*, I received a lot of e-mails asking about rookie running backs. The most common topic is how to project rookies—something I'll touch on later—but I always respond that gambling on certain rookie running backs is often a wise move. Whereas rookie wide receivers rarely post outstanding fantasy numbers, rookie runners have the ability to step right in and become relevant in the world of fantasy football.

Fantasy owners hate the unknown. Rookie running backs, who are accompanied by bigger question marks than most other backs, can sometimes offer good value because there is so much uncertainty surrounding them.

- **The Numbers on Rookie Running Backs**

It isn't as if all rookie running backs provide value. Actually, the majority of rookie runners finish lower than their preseason average draft position. I tracked all rookie running backs drafted in the first three rounds of the NFL Draft since 2006, and only 36.6 percent finished their rookie seasons in a spot ahead of their average draft position. That is, almost two-thirds of all rookie running backs perform below expectations.

Further, the average fantasy draft position of rookie running backs selected in Rounds 1, 2, and 3 of the NFL Draft has been 41.7 among all players at the position. Their average final rank among running backs has been just 50.2.

So why the hell would I suggest drafting them? The reason is that, with the exception of a few Trent Richardson-type players, rookie running backs rarely get selected in the first few rounds. Since 2006, the average draft position of the top rookie running back off of the board has been just 19th. Only Ryan Mathews in 2010 cracked the top 10. Darren McFadden (18th) and Reggie Bush (14th) were the only other running backs to get selected in the top 20 of all running backs in their rookie seasons.

In the middle and especially late rounds of drafts, your goal should be acquiring upside. It can be a deathblow to your fantasy team if your first pick fizzles out, but it isn't too much of an issue if your 14th-round pick is a bust. Thus, there's no reason to play it safe; you should seek players with very high ceilings late in the draft.

Perhaps no late-round picks have provided the upside of rookie running backs over the past half-decade. Despite only three rookie runners getting selected in the top 20 running backs over that time, nine (Chris Johnson, Matt Forte, Kevin Smith, Steve Slaton, Adrian Peterson, Marshawn Lynch, Reggie

Bush, Joseph Addai, and Maurice Jones-Drew) have finished in the top 20 by season's end. Seven of those nine have actually finished in the top 12 running backs, making them legitimate No. 1 players at the position.

How about the value of some of these picks:

Chris Johnson: ADP 36, Final Rank 11
Matt Forte: ADP 28, Final Rank 4
Kevin Smith: ADP 30, Final Rank 18
Steve Slaton: ADP 47, Final Rank 6
Adrian Peterson: ADP 25, Final Rank 3
Marshawn Lynch: ADP 24, Final Rank 12
Joseph Addai: ADP 27, Final Rank 11
Maurice Jones-Drew: ADP 62, Final Rank 8

It's almost impossible to think some of those running backs were selected as low as they were. Adrian Peterson was the 25th running back off of the board in his rookie season? Maurice Jones-Drew was 62nd? Wow.

For the record, I tracked the production of all running backs during the same time period. It turns out rookie running backs selected lower than 30th at the position are about *four times as likely* to finish in the top 20 as other running backs drafted in the same range.

Ultimately, rookie running backs are high-risk/high-reward options. In the middle and late rounds where they tend to get drafted, that sort of volatility is *exactly* what you want.

- ### The Bottom Line

In the late rounds, rookie running backs are the way to go. Because of their ability to contribute immediately, late-round rookie running backs are four times as likely to break out as others break out at the position. Meanwhile, you'll be hard-pressed to find production from rookie receivers or tight ends, especially in the late rounds.

10 Are rookie quarterbacks the new rookie running backs?

Chris Johnson, Matt Forte, Maurice Jones-Drew, Doug Martin. Shrewd fantasy owners have known for years that rookie running backs have the potential to offer unbelievable value. Even today, the uncertainty that surrounds first-year backs is often the impetus for dropping them in rankings, even if isn't as significant of a drop as in past years.

Recently, though, we've seen rookie quarterbacks absolutely skyrocket in the final fantasy rankings. It began in 2011 with Cam Newton and Andy Dalton. Dalton's 17th place finish might seem trivial, but it was actually the highest for a rookie quarterback since Matt Ryan's 13th place finish in 2008. Of course, Newton stole the show, using a combination of his legs and rocket arm to finish fourth among quarterbacks in most scoring formats. The results were unprecedented.

In 2012, the trend has continued with Robert Griffin III (sixth) and Andrew Luck (ninth). Heck, even Russell Wilson finished No. 11. The question for fantasy owners is whether or not the recent rise of the rookie quarterback is a natural progression of the position—one that has arisen from colleges preparing rookies to play in the NFL immediately—or simply the result of a unique group of select passers finding unusual first-year success over just a two-year period.

In terms of any sort of trend, the improvement in rookie quarterback production has been dramatic, not a gradual increase.

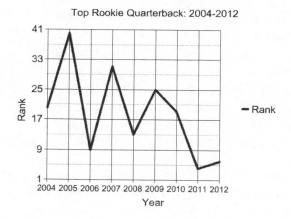

Top Rookie Quarterback: 2004-2012

From 2004 to 2010, there was no consistent trend among rookie quarterback fantasy production. The top rookie quarterback over that period was Vince Young with a ninth-place finish in 2006. On average, though, the best rookie quarterback each season averaged just a 25th-place finish, meaning first-year quarterbacks weren't even really worthy of a selection in redraft leagues.

With three rookie quarterbacks in the last two seasons—Newton, Griffin, and Luck—finishing in the top 10 at the position in their first year, though, it sure seems like things have changed. Could such a dramatic jump really be the result of chance?

While there's certainly an element of randomness at work (meaning the quality of the quarterbacks in the last two draft classes has been unusually phenomenal), we're also seeing a shift in the way quarterbacks are being used. What do Newton, Griffin, Luck, and Wilson have in common? They were all highly-drafted quarterbacks who can run. That's a valuable combination for fantasy owners. All three players have been able to rely on their legs when things break down or, even better, they have run plays—read-options and bootlegs—called specifically for them to gash defenses on the ground.

Actually, Newton, Griffin, Luck, and Wilson have all been historically great runners at the quarterback position. In 2011, Newton totaled more rushing yards-per-game than all but five quarterbacks since 1990. He also broke the record for rushing touchdowns by a quarterback, and by a wide margin. Actually, only five quarterbacks over the past two decades have totaled even half of Newton's 14 rushing touchdowns in his rookie season.

Griffin is like Michael Vick with superior passing ability. RGIII's rookie decision-making was unbelievable and he also rushed for the fifth-most yards-per-game for a quarterback since 1990. Luck, although not as adept on the ground as the others, still finished with five rushing touchdowns. Wilson's 489 rushing yards rank him in the top 25 for any quarterback in the past two decades.

Thus, while you still need to be careful drafting rookie quarterbacks, look out for those taken high in the NFL Draft who can run. Chances are you'll be able to grab future rookie passers, regardless of their skill set, as your No. 2 quarterback. With such little risk, rookie quarterbacks can certainly be worth your attention; you just need to know where to look.

• The Bottom Line

Although luck has been part of the equation, rookie quarterbacks are more equipped than ever to succeed during their first year in the NFL. The past two seasons have been remarkable, highlighted by talented dual-threat quarterbacks. Mobile rookie quarterbacks now generally offer tremendous value as your No. 2 option.

11 Do rookie tight ends offer any value?

In 2010, then-rookie tight end Rob Gronkowski erupted for double-digit touchdowns on his way to a fifth-place finish among all tight ends. That occurrence is probably rarer than you think; in the past seven years, Gronkowski is the only rookie tight end to finish as a top 12 option at the position. For whatever reason, first-year tight ends simply don't produce like some other rookies.

Check out the final ranks of the top rookie tight ends since 2006.

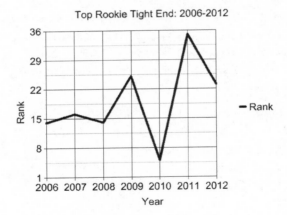

You can see that Gronkowski is an outlier in a group whose average is only 19th place. The list also includes Brandon Pettigrew, Dustin Keller, Owen

Daniels, Zach Miller, Kyle Rudolph, and Dwayne Allen.

With no rookie tight end in the top 20 in the past two seasons, one has to wonder whether it's becoming more difficult for rookies to make an early impact for their squads. With tight ends getting integrated into offenses more and more each season, it's possible that it's taking rookies longer to learn the nuances of the position. Plus, the job responsibilities of most tight ends include things other than catching the football—actually, they're probably the most versatile of any position—making the jump to the big leagues a challenging one.

Of course, it's also possible that the last two draft classes have simply been poor at the tight end position, resulting in lower fantasy ranks. Top pick Coby Fleener wasn't drafted until the second round in 2012. The next tight end off of the board—Allen— became Fleener's teammate in Indianapolis but wasn't drafted until the third round.

Rudolph was the top tight end in 2011, but he too wasn't drafted until the second round. Lance Kendricks and Rob Housler rounded out one of the weakest trios of tight ends in recent memory. Prior to 2011, the last time a tight end failed to get drafted in the first round was 1999, and now it's happened in back-to-back seasons.

Overall, there were only six total tight ends taken in the first three rounds in 2011 and 2012. In comparison, there were nearly seven per year in the three prior seasons. In 2008, we witnessed an elite tight end class with Dustin Keller, John Carlson, Fred Davis, Martellus Bennett, Jermichael Finley, and Jacob Tamme among the names called. All of those players have gone on to become starters in the world of fantasy football, yet none of them were able to finish in the top 12 at the tight end position in their rookie seasons.

While rookie running backs continue to dominate and rookie quarterbacks are moving up the ranks, first-year tight ends simply aren't getting it done. The last two drafts have been unusually weak, but rookie tight ends have still been notoriously poor fantasy options. Unless you're fairly certain you have a Gronkowski on your hands, it's probably best to avoid rookie tight ends completely.

- **The Bottom Line**

Simply put, rookie tight ends rarely produce. Avoid them at all costs, especially with another weak 2013 class.

12 How do you pick the best free agents on the waiver wire after Week 1?

In a game with so much inherent luck, fantasy football is often won or lost with "the little things." You need to hit on a good number of your draft picks, of course, but starting the correct player one week or picking up the best free agent another week can really be the difference between a fantasy championship and missing the playoffs entirely.

The strategies employed with in-season moves, such as waiver wire acquisitions, are often far different from those during the draft. Whereas much of the draft is an attempt to uncover a "sure thing," there are no such guarantees on the waiver wire. Your goal isn't to find a can't-miss player, but rather to maximize your chances of hitting on what will likely turn out to be a dud. You're truly sifting for a diamond in the rough.

I tracked the top 20 Week 1 waiver wire pickups (in terms of how often they were added) each year since 2008. Of those players, just 25 percent went on to produce starter-quality numbers on the season (in leagues that start one quarterback, two running backs, three receivers, and one tight end). Waiver wire pickups can often hold down the fort for a few weeks while a starter is injured or, more likely, add a few points as a capable bye week fill-in. For the most part, however, even the top free agents in fantasy football—those picked up after the first week of the season—don't produce relevant fantasy stats.

Of course, picking up players early in the season isn't generally about finding replacement players. Often, owners try to stash potential "gold" that could hit it big down the road—a backup running back, for example. In that sense, you want to seek the players at positions with the greatest odds to produce every-week starter numbers.

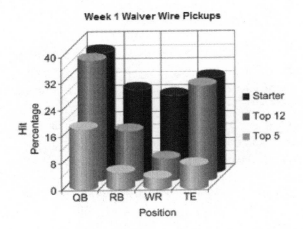

Week 1 Waiver Wire Pickups

And since 2008, no position has been more productive than quarterback. Of the most-added Week 1 free agent quarterbacks over the past four seasons, over one-in-three turns into a top 12 player at the position. Right around one-in-six finishes in the top five among all signal-callers. That's serious upside. We see similar production from the tight ends. Just under one-in-three of Week 1 pickups have turned into top 12 players.

One of the reasons that free agent quarterbacks and tight ends have been able to produce is that there are simply better options left on waivers. In many leagues, there are a handful of owners with just a single quarterback or tight end on their rosters. That leaves players like the 2010 version of Marcedes Lewis on the free agent pile.

Meanwhile, the running back and wide receiver positions get overstocked. Yeah, you start more players at each position, but there's no reason to have seven wide receivers on your roster if you own just a single quarterback. Fewer than one-in-four of the top early-season free agent receivers finish in the top 36 at their position. Brandon Lloyd in 2010 is the only case of an undrafted receiver finishing in the top 10.

As far as running backs go, the abundance of injuries at the position increases the overall upside of free agents. Free agent running backs are about twice as likely as free agent receivers to end up as top 12 players at their respective positions. The downside is that everyone knows when injuries occur. Thus, your odds of striking gold on a free agent running back are primarily influenced by luck, i.e. your waiver position, whereas finding a stud quarterback or tight end on waivers is more about playing the percentages.

You can see that, historically, quarterbacks have been the best waiver wire additions, with 36.4 percent of the top performers in Week 1 turning into top 12 quarterbacks by season's end. I think the success of free agent quarterbacks is to be expected because 1) with 32 NFL starters, there is less competition, and 2) a lot of the pickups were the result of injuries to starters. Of the top quarterbacks picked up on waivers since 2008, only Cam Newton's addition really came as the result of a great performance in Week 1. Matt Cassel in 2008 and Michael Vick in 2010 were priority waiver wire acquisitions simply because of injuries to Tom Brady and Kevin Kolb, respectively.

The success of free agent tight ends (28.6 percent of the top Week 1 performers became fantasy starters), like that of the signal-callers, is likely due to an abundance of free agent options. Most owners draft just a single tight end, leaving players like Marcedes Lewis (fourth in 2010) and John Carlson (seventh in 2008) in the free agent pool. Still, the reasoning for quality free agents doesn't really matter—you can find respectable players at the tight end position.

Contrary to popular belief, running back and wide receiver additions haven't been as profitable for fantasy owners as the other two skill positions. Since 2008, just a single wide receiver that went undrafted in the majority of fantasy leagues (Brandon Lloyd in 2010) finished in the top 10 at the position.

Meanwhile, free agent running backs Steve Slaton (2008), Jamaal Charles (2009), and Peyton Hillis (2010) all finished in the top 12 among all players at their position, making them No. 1 fantasy options. The running back pool isn't deep, but you have a greater chance of striking gold there than at wide receiver.

• What about rookie free agents?

Quarterbacks

Outside of Cam Newton's historical 2011 season, it's extremely rare for a rookie quarterback to be relevant in the fantasy football world. Tom Brady, Peyton Manning, Matthew Stafford, Drew Brees— none of them came close to dominating the fantasy football rankings as a first-year player. The nature of the game is changing and rookie passers are certainly more prepared to play than ever before, but those first-year players are typically gone after your draft. If you're looking to rookie free agent quarterbacks to bolster you fantasy lineup, you might be in trouble.

Wide Receivers

While uncovering a wide receiver gem on the waiver wire is rare, finding a rookie stud at the position is next to impossible. Since 2006, only six rookie wide outs have finished in the top 24 players at their position. Three of those—A.J. Green, Julio Jones, and Torrey Smith—were rookies in 2011. And as first-round selections in the 2011 NFL Draft, you sure weren't claiming those guys off of waivers.

Further, only one rookie wide receiver (Mike Williams in 2010) finished in the top 12 over that time. One! Williams and Eddie Royal (2008) have been the only two rookie wide receivers who you could have legitimately picked up on waivers to provide you with decent fantasy numbers in the past six seasons.

Tight Ends

Rob Gronkowski finished fifth in fantasy points as a rookie in 2010, and John Carlson was seventh in 2008. No other tight ends since 2006 have finished in the top 12 at the position. That rookie tight end taken in the seventh round of the NFL Draft that you think could go nuts in 2012 isn't the next Gronkowski. Well, maybe he's the next *Chris* Gronkowski.

Running Backs

I saved this position for last because it's the only one where you can find legitimate rookie talent. Just in the last five years, nine rookie running backs have finished in the top 20 at their position. Almost all of them were either selected late in fantasy drafts or went undrafted completely. Chris Johnson, Steve Slaton, and Maurice Jones-Drew are a few examples of rookie running backs that lit it up despite rarely getting drafted in fantasy football.

- ## The Bottom Line

In searching for the perfect Week 1 waiver wire pickup, you're goal should be maximizing upside. For that, quarterback and tight end are the most natural fits. If you're seeking a running back, go with a rookie who could potentially see a heavy workload at some point during the year.

13 Are rookie wide receivers worth drafting?

In 2011, a trio of rookie wide receivers—A.J. Green, Julio Jones, and Torrey Smith—finished in the top 23 in fantasy points among all receivers. That doesn't sound too amazing, does it? Well perhaps you should ramp up your excitement level, because the odds of three rookie wide receivers finishing so high are a lot smaller than you might think.

For years, I used to gamble on rookie wide receivers late in drafts because I thought they possessed a ton of upside. I mean, what wasn't to love about Chad Jackson in the 13th round? Oh, now wait, don't answer that.

The truth is that rookie receivers don't have as high of ceilings as you might believe. Last year was a major aberration in the world of fantasy football. Since 2000, only one other rookie receiver has finished in the top 20 at his position. Can you guess who it was? If you said Mike Williams, you'd be correct. He finished 11th among receivers in 2011.

Those four players—Green, Jones, Smith, and Williams—join Eddie Royal as the only five rookie receivers that could even be considered No. 2 fantasy options in their first years in the NFL. And considering you probably would have been pretty unlikely to start those players in the first few weeks of the season, that doesn't leave you with too many fantasy points.

It isn't as if rookie receivers are drastically underperforming. Over the last half-decade, the average fantasy draft position of the top five rookie receivers (in terms of where they were selected in the NFL Draft) is 61st at the position. Together, those 25 players have combined to finish 68th in their rookie years among all receivers. On average, you basically get what you pay for with a rookie receiver.

The problem is that rookie wide receivers get selected late in drafts. Actually, the ADP of the top rookie receivers in each of the last five fantasy drafts has been only 34th at the position. Your goal in the late rounds of fantasy drafts is no longer risk minimization; instead, it should be maximizing upside.

Rookie receivers *seem* like the natural choice, but they surprisingly don't possess the upside you covet. To show that 2011 (and Williams in 2010) were outliers, take a look at the top (other) rookie wide receiver from previous seasons:

2010: Dez Bryant (49th)
2009: Percy Harvin (25th)
2008: Eddie Royal (20th)
2007: Dwayne Bowe (24th)
2006: Santonio Holmes (41st)

And these are the best of the best. For every Eddie Royal, there are three Devin Thomas-type players.

You might think that all rookies see these kinds of numbers, but you'd be wrong. Since 2006, seven rookie running backs have finished in the top 12 at the position. That's seven running backs ahead of the top rookie receiver in over a decade (Green). Three of those rookie running backs—Chris Johnson, Steve Slaton, and Adrian Peterson—even finished in the top six among all runners.

So while your league-mates are gambling on rookie receivers late in drafts this year, do yourself a favor and bypass the youngsters for a player with more upside. Chances are a rookie running back will provide a whole lot more bang for your buck.

● **The Bottom Line**
Your chances of hitting on a rookie receiver are slim. The ones that post respectable numbers are still usually over-drafted. There's simply not much value in first-year receivers, and avoiding them altogether isn't a bad strategy.

14 Do players perform better during contract seasons?

If July is the time that the most diehard of fantasy football owners create their initial projections and rankings, August is the season for getting bombarded with football "truisms" that often turn out to be anything but, you know, true. "Player X is a wide receiver in his third season and I remember a third-year receiver who broke out once." Okay, cool.

One of the fantasy football rules-of-thumb you're bound to hear again and again this year is to target players in contract years. According to many fantasy football analysts, players entering the final year of their contracts have extra motivation to cash in and will thus post outstanding fantasy numbers.

On the surface, the idea seems to make sense. And if it *seems* like it could be true, eventually it will "become" true within the world of fantasy football. Fantasy owners and experts will search for confirming instances of players in contract years lighting it up, and they'll find plenty of such occurrences. They'll see Marshawn Lynch's 2011 outburst, Ahmad Bradshaw's big 2010 season, and Maurice Jones-Drew's 2009 breakout campaign. Ah, three confirmations of a very grandiose, overarching idea. It *must* be true.

It's very easy to remember instances that confirm a hypothesis. When one high-powered fantasy expert claims that NFL players exceed expectations in contract years, fantasy owners accept that idea and then look for occurrences that confirm their new belief. Often times, it isn't even a conscious decision.

For every Lynch, Bradshaw, and Jones-Drew, however, there is a Derrick Ward in 2008, T.J. Houshmandzadeh in the same season, and DeSean Jackson in 2011—all players who underachieved in a contract year. It's easy to forget information that negates a hypothesis, but when it comes to NFL players in contract seasons, it appears as though underachieving is just as common as its counterpart.

I did some research on the fantasy performances of NFL players in contract years since 2008. To make an assessment of their play in their contract seasons as accurate as possible, I compared their performances to their production in the previous two seasons. Exceptions included players who were injured for an extensive portion of one of the prior seasons and players whose workload recently shifted dramatically. For the most part, though, the data includes just about every contract year player from the past five seasons.

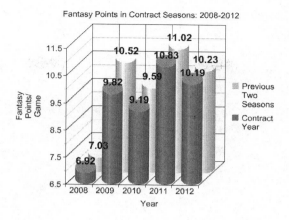

Fantasy Points in Contract Seasons: 2008-2012

You can see that the fantasy points-per-game of players in contract years have been remarkably similar to their production in the two seasons prior to their contract seasons. Actually, their fantasy output has actually been slightly lower than anticipated in every season since 2008. The difference isn't statistically significant, but the results indicate that there's no real motivational factor that causes NFL players to produce superior numbers in contract years.

Let's go further and break down the results by position. . .

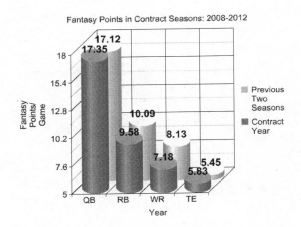

Fantasy Points in Contract Seasons: 2008-2012

Regardless of position, the production of players in their contract years matches up extremely well with their stats from the previous two seasons. No matter how you slice it, NFL players simply don't overachieve in contract seasons.

Now, you might be wondering how the play of the league's most elite players changes in contract years. I broke down the results based on players who scored a minimum of 10 fantasy points-per-game in the two seasons prior to their contract years, and the results are still the same; the best fantasy producers actually scored more points prior to their contract seasons (13.98) than during their contract years (12.87).

And as if the results weren't conclusive enough, consider that over half of the players assessed scored more points-per-game in the two years before their contract season than in it. That's about as obvious as it can get; NFL players, over large sample sizes, will play exactly the same in contract seasons as they did before them.

So when you hear a fantasy analyst touting a player because he's in a contract year, you will know that the player's fantasy stock may be artificially inflated because of a factor that simply has no measurable effect on performance.

- ## The Bottom Line

If you think that targeting contract-year players will provide value, think again. On average, contract-year players produce at just about the same rate as players who aren't in the final year of their deals. That goes for every position and every skill level. There's no reason to avoid contract-year players, but there's no reason to specifically go after them, either.

15 How do you project a running back's yards-per-carry?

One of the most difficult tasks in projecting fantasy football statistics is determining which aspects of players' games are repeatable, and which are a matter of luck. That is, what percentage of Calvin Johnson's 1,964 receiving yards in 2012 were due to skill and other factors that are likely to repeat in 2012? The more luck that was involved with Johnson's receiving totals, the more likely they are to regress this season.

Rather than simply arbitrarily guessing projections, there are formulas we can use to make more educated predictions (albeit still "guesses") regarding players' stats. To show just how much of an impact a regression-toward-the-mean analysis can have and exactly how to implement it into your projections, let's take a look at how to project running backs' yards-per-carry.

The formula I will use is a basic one, but it can be applied to all rate statistics to effectively factor in regression. Remember, 'regression toward the mean' is the tendency for measurements to occur closer to the mean than they did previously. Adrian Peterson is an amazing running back, but we'd never expect him to repeat his 2012 season in 2013. Rate stats like yards-per-carry, yards-per-reception, drop rate, and so on can all be projected rather easily with this approach.

The most taxing aspect of creating rate-based projections is uncovering the strength of correlation for year-to-year stats, i.e. the average percentage of each individual player's numbers that transfers over to subsequent seasons.

I did some work and found a strength of correlation of right around 0.41 for running backs' YPC over the half decade. For our purposes, that means that 41 percent of a running back's YPC is due to skill, and the other 59 percent is due to fluky factors, such as opponents, field conditions, and so on. For other rate statistics, the most difficult aspect of the analysis, and the majority of your work, is spent uncovering the strength of correlation between Year X and Year X+1.

After all is said and done, we can accurately predict running backs' YPC with the following formula:

$$YPC\_x+1 = 0.59*(AvgYPC) + 0.41*(YPC\_x)$$

In layman's terms, this means multiplying the league average YPC (around 4.30) by 0.59, then adding it to the player's YPC from the previous season (which is multiplied by 0.41).

Let's say a running back averaged 5.03 YPC. To obtain a baseline projection for the following season, you first multiply 5.03 by 0.41 (getting 2.06 as a result). Then, you multiply the league average YPC (4.30) by 0.59 to get 2.54. Adding the two figures together, you'll find that a baseline projection for a running back coming off of a season with 5.03 YPC is 4.60 YPC.

Note that I call this number a baseline projection. There is more that goes into predicting statistics than just this formula, it gives us a foundation from which to work. When projecting other rate statistics, you can see a lower strength of correlation from year to year will result in greater regression toward the mean. If a statistic hypothetically had zero predictive ability, we would multiply the league average by 1.00, leaving every player with the exact same projection. Hello kickers!

- **The Bottom Line**

The formula to project a running back's YPC is $YPC\_x+1 = 0.59*(AvgYPC) + 0.41*(YPC\_x)$. That's a complicated way of saying that 59 percent of a running back's efficiency is due to luck and only 41 percent is the result of skill. Since the league-average YPC is right around 4.30, you can obtain a baseline projection for any running back by multiplying his past YPC by 0.41, then adding it to 2.54. A simplified version of the formula would be $YPC = 2.54 + 0.41*(Past\ YPC)$.

16 Which second-year running backs break out?

As fantasy owners, our primary goal is to acquire players whose actual worth exceeds their perceived value. Like stock traders, fantasy owners can garner a competitive advantage by leveraging knowledge about how a player (or stock) will perform in the future relative to their past production.

Often times, young players provide a hefty return on investment because they haven't been in position to post stellar stats in their short careers. This is one reason why rookie running backs tend to get undervalued far too much. Doug Martin of the Tampa Bay Bucs was one of the best values in fantasy drafts in 2012, and that was because owners were scared to take on the perceived risk that accompanies him.

Of course, projecting rookies is an extremely difficult task. With no past NFL production to use as a predictor for future success, fantasy owners are often less simply guessing how rookies will perform. Second-year players, on the other hand, have at least a small body of work that we can utilize to make predictions.

I recently collected some numbers on running backs to see if there are any stats from rookie seasons that can accurately predict future NFL success. I used career approximate value (AV) as a gauge of fantasy worth, tracking the top 40 running backs in this measure since 2000. Then, I compared their rookie stats with their future production.

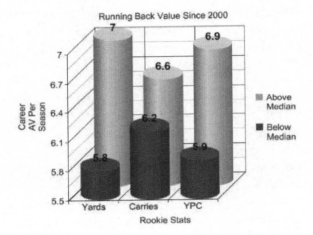

You can see that running backs who post the most rushing yards in their rookie seasons generally go on to have the most career success. The top 20 running backs in terms of rookie rushing yards posted an AV-per-season of 7.0, compared to just 5.8 for the bottom 20 running backs in terms of rushing yards.

That result isn't really a surprise, however. As a general rule of thumb, we'd expect the best rookie running backs to rush for the most yards simply because they're given the most opportunities. We knew that Trent Richardson would be among the leading rookie rushers in 2012 simply because we knew he would see a heavy workload. On top of that, since rushing yards contribute to AV, there's a bit of a selection bias at work, i.e. the numbers will naturally be skewed toward backs with a lot of rushing yards in their rookie seasons.

I think there is more evidence that rookie rushing yards aren't as accurate of a predictor of NFL success as the graph shows in the form of the stats on carries. If a heavy rookie workload were a cause of future success, we'd see a greater gap between the top 20 and bottom 20 running backs in terms of carries.

In reality, I think yards-per-carry is the most accurate predictor of future NFL success at the running back position. YPC isn't factored into AV, so there's no selection bias inherent to the results. The fact that the career AV of the most efficient rookie running backs (in terms of YPC) is even close to that of the most productive rookie running backs (in terms of yards) is really quite amazing.

- **How to Use the Numbers**

The best way to predict the career success of second-year running backs is to assess both their rookie YPC and rushing yards. Even though YPC is probably superior to yards in terms of determining a running backs' talent, yards are still strongly correlated to future success. You always want talented players, but there's no substitute for a heavy workload.

When drafting second-year running backs, here is what to consider (in order):

- **Rookie YPC**
- **Rookie rushing yards**
- **Draft spot**

All other things being equal, I'm going to select second-year running backs who were extremely efficient in their rookie seasons. Rushing yards should also be a consideration, and you can really use a combination of the two stats. Finally, look at where each back was drafted. You can put up with a lower YPC a little bit more if a player was drafted highly because you know his team will stick by him longer. Trent Richardson didn't post great efficiency 2012, for example, but he'll still be the Browns' starter in 2013.

2013 Second-Year Running Backs

- **Trent Richardson: #3 Pick – 247 carries for 869 yards (3.5 YPC)**
- **Doug Martin: #31 Pick – 264 carries for 1,234 yards (4.7 YPC)**
- **David Wilson: #32 Pick – 41 carries for 211 yards (5.1 YPC)**
- **Ronnie Hillman: #67 Pick – 61 carries for 250 yards (4.1 YPC)**

- **Bernard Pierce: #84 Pick** – 67 carries for 300 yards (4.5 YPC)
- **Robert Turbin: #106 Pick** – 65 carries for 290 yards (4.5 YPC)
- **Vick Ballard: #170 Pick** – 146 carries for 562 yards (3.8 YPC)
- **Alfred Morris: #173 Pick** – 253 carries for 1,228 yards (4.9 YPC)
- **Bryce Brown: #229 Pick** – 87 carries for 494 yards (5.7 YPC)
- **Daryl Richardson: #252 Pick** – 88 carries for 461 yards (5.2 YPC)

A few observations. . .

- Trent Richardson is surprisingly the worst rookie on the list in terms of YPC. The Browns' offense doesn't help and Richardson will get plenty of chances to rack up points in future years, but it's something to keep in the back of your mind.
- The ideal candidate as a 2013 breakout player would be a highly-drafted running back without a lot of production but high efficiency in his rookie season. That description fits David Wilson perfectly, and you can bet his preseason ranking, at least on my board, will exceed his ADP.
- Alfred Morris has obviously been extremely efficient with Robert Griffin III taking pressure off of him. There's not really a

major reason to avoid Morris in 2013, but his ADP may end up being a bit too high for any Shanahan-coached running back simply because you never know if he'll get pulled.

- Bryce Brown is such an intriguing player in 2013 because he's been absolutely remarkable in his rookie year, but he has LeSean McCoy ahead of him. It will be a situation to monitor in training camp next year.

- Even with Willis McGahee's career nearing its end, be cautious with Ronnie Hillman. He's effectively been replaced by Knowshon Moreno this year and the rookie has been rather inefficient with his 61 carries.

- Give Daryl Richardson a long look in 2013. Steven Jackson has handled nearly three times as many carries as Richardson, yet averaged 1.3 yards less per rush. Jackson is beginning to get phased out of St. Louis's long-term plans, and Richardson won't cost you much next season as a seventh-round pick in the 2012 NFL Draft.

- **The Bottom Line**

If you're looking for value on second-year running backs, search for efficiency. A player like David Wilson—who averaged 5.0 YPC during his rookie season—is the prototypical target because he was efficient without posting huge bulk stats. Since bulk stats like total yards and touchdowns get factored into a player's draft position but YPC doesn't hold as much weight, you can acquire value by "paying" for YPC for second-year running backs.

17 How do you project wide receivers with rookie stats?

Although consensus fantasy football rankings have improved dramatically over the past few years, the general public still overpays for bulk stats. That is, owners generally draft players who have already posted respectable fantasy numbers over those who have yet to produce. That's not necessarily a bad thing, of course; all other things equal, you'd obviously prefer a "sure thing" over an unknown commodity. Having said that, one of the easiest ways to acquire value in fantasy football drafts is to identify those players on the verge of breaking out—the players in the Dez Bryant/Demaryius Thomas mold whose past production doesn't properly reflect their potential output.

Let's consider second-year running backs. When everyone else is paying for carries and yards, look for second-year backs who were highly efficient in their first year, yet didn't necessarily produce big-time fantasy numbers. David Wilson will be a perfect example of such a player in 2013; he'll likely move up boards, but even so he'll be extremely likely to outperform his ADP.

One of the reasons that rookie running backs with high YPC have generally superior careers to those first-year backs with lots of carries and yards is that rookie runners are capable of coming into the NFL and playing well immediately. We've seen that over the past decade with backs such as Doug Martin, Adrian Peterson, Matt Forte, Maurice Jones-Drew, and so on. Since rookie running backs don't necessarily need an elite level of talent to rush for a lot of yards, the value we place on rookie rushing yards should be limited; we see backs like Steve Slaton kill it in their first year before fading away.

It's a lot different for rookie wide receivers. As I've mentioned, only six rookie wide receivers have finished in the top 24 at their position since 2000. Simply put, rookie wide receivers rarely provide meaningful contributions to fantasy owners. That means that when a rookie wide out produces at even the level of a No. 2 wide receiver—as A.J. Green, Julio Jones, and Torrey Smith all did in 2011—it's typically reflective of a higher cutoff of talent than is the case for rookie running backs, and thus a sign of long-term success.

The Numbers on Rookie Receivers

The stats back up that idea. As I did with running backs, I tracked the top rookie wide receivers since 2000 in terms of both efficiency and bulk metrics: receptions, yards, yards-per-catch, and touchdowns. I then calculated the average approximate value—an excellent gauge of overall fantasy value—for the rookie receivers ranked highest in each category.

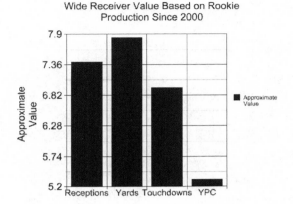

Wide Receiver Value Based on Rookie Production Since 2000

The numbers aren't even close; receptions and yards are the best predictors of future NFL success for rookie wide receivers. Touchdowns are a close third, but yards-per-catch is way, way down the list. That's the exact opposite of rookie running backs; for them, yards-per-carry is more predictive of future fantasy value than both carries and yards.

It's worth noting that yards and touchdowns are functions of approximate value, so we'd expect those stats to contribute to their total AV a bit. Still, that fact can't come close to accounting for the vast gap in AV between rookies with high bulk stats and those with great efficiency. Plus, remember that the same is true for rookie running backs, yet their efficiency still proved to be a greater predictor of future value than bulk numbers.

2013 Second-Year Wide Receivers

There's a widespread notion that wide receivers break out in their third seasons, but I think their second year in the league is really the time to pounce. If you're in a keeper league, especially, it's better to secure a few second-year receivers at a low price tag than waiting until their third year when you'll likely get into a bidding war of sorts for their services.

Ultimately, any rookie wide receiver that posts respectable stats is at least worthy of consideration in their second season. And since rookie wide receivers almost never finish even as No. 2 options at their position, you won't really be hindered by "paying" for bulk stats in the same way that you'll have to spend an arm and a leg for many second-year running backs; you'll need to use a first-round pick to secure someone like Doug Martin or Trent Richardson in 2013, yet the top second-year receivers may not get drafted in the first four or five rounds.

Let's take a look at some of the interesting rookie wide receivers this year. . .

- **Justin Blackmon: #5 Pick – 64 receptions for 865 yards, 5 TD**
- **Michael Floyd: #13 Pick – 45 receptions for 562 yards, 2 TD**

- Kendall Wright: #20 Pick – 64 receptions for 626 yards, 4 TD
- A.J. Jenkins: #30 Pick – 0 receptions
- Brian Quick: #33 Pick – 11 receptions for 156 yards, 2 TD
- Stephen Hill: #43 Pick – 21 receptions for 252 yards, 3 TD
- Alshon Jeffery: #45 Pick – 24 receptions for 367 yards, 3 TD
- Ryan Broyles: #54 Pick – 22 receptions for 310 yards, 2 TD
- T.J. Graham: #69 Pick – 31 receptions, 322 yards, 1 TD
- Mohamed Sanu: #83 Pick – 16 receptions, 154 yards, 4 TD
- T.Y. Hilton: #92 Pick – 50 receptions for 861 yards, 7 TD
- Chris Givens: #96 Pick – 42 receptions for 698 yards, 3 TD
- Josh Gordon: Supplemental Draft – 50 receptions, 805 yards, 5 TD

Since receptions, yards, and touchdowns are the best indicators of future value at the wide receiver position, your second-year receiver rankings probably won't differ too much from consensus rankings. However, you can potentially secure value by upgrading the big producers from this class as a whole.

While others are passing on receivers like Gordon and Blackmon because of scary quarterback situations, you can jump on two of the more prominent rookie wide outs, both of whom are a decent quarterback away from legit No. 1 wide receiver potential over the next decade.

- **The Bottom Line**

Like rookie running backs, second-year receivers can really offer a solid return on your investment. That's because they typically see major boosts in during their second year, but you'll be paying for their moderate rookie production. Emphasize bulk stats—the ones that score you fantasy points—over efficiency when searching for second-year wide receivers.

18 Which second-year tight ends are worth a gamble?

The 2012 NFL Draft was only the second time since 1999 that no tight end was selected in the first round. Stanford's Coby Fleener was the first player at the position to come off the board in the beginning of the second round, and his current teammate on the Colts—Clemson's Dwayne Allen— was the next tight end to get drafted all the way in the third round.

The weak rookie tight end class didn't do much of anything in 2012. Of course, that can be a good thing for fantasy owners, too. Since tight ends take time to develop, grabbing them during their second seasons can offer value. I broke down the stats of rookie tight ends since 2000 to see which are most predictive of future NFL success.

If you recall, different stats are important when projecting players at various positions. Efficiency is key for running backs, for example; yards-per-carry is a far better indicator of future NFL success even than yards or carries for rookie runners. On the other hand, efficiency for wide receivers (as measured by yards-per-reception) is almost meaningless.

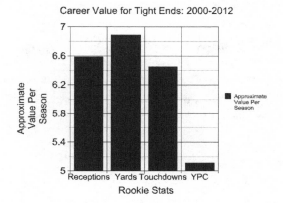

Career Value for Tight Ends: 2000-2012

Rookie tight ends are much like wide receivers; yards-per-catch is a rather poor predictor of future value. It's the bulk stats—catches, yards, and touchdowns—that matter for tight ends. Interestingly, all three stats count about the same.

When I discussed the successes of quarterbacks, I mentioned that draft spot plays a large role in projecting second-year signal-callers. Whereas mid and even late-round wide receivers and running backs, especially, often thrive in the NFL, the majority of elite quarterbacks were selected in the first round. There are the JaMarcus Russell first-round busts and the Tom Brady late-round hits, but those are exceptions to the rule.

The same is true for tight ends; you might strike gold on an Antonio Gates from time to time, but betting on tight ends who were drafted early is generally a winning proposition. Of the top 20 tight ends in approximate value since 2000, over half of them were drafted in the first round. That's pretty remarkable when you consider that only 16 tight ends have even been drafted in the first round since 2000. That's a 62.5 percent chance of finding an elite or near-elite player simply by using the NFL Draft as a guide.

2013 Second-Year Tight Ends

To project the second-year tight ends in 2013, let's take a look at the stats of some of the top rookies in 2012.

- **Coby Fleener: #34 Pick, 26 receptions for 281 yards, 2 TD**
- **Dwayne Allen: #64 Pick, 45 receptions for 521 yards, 3 TD**
- **Ladarius Green: #110 Pick, 4 receptions for 56 yards, 0 TD**
- **Orson Charles: #116 Pick, 8 receptions for 101 yards, 0 TD**
- **James Hanna: #186 Pick, 8 receptions for 86 yards, 0 TD**

You can see that there simply won't be many second-year tight end options for owners in 2013. The top two picks from 2012—Fleener and Allen—led the class by a wide margin, and they both play on the same team.

I mentioned that there have been only two seasons since 1999 in which a tight end wasn't drafted in the first round. Well, the other season was just last year, meaning we haven't had a first-round tight end since Jermaine Gresham in 2010. Of course, Fleener was drafted just after the first round, and it isn't like a player selected after the initial 32 picks is magically going to perform worse because he dropped two spots.

The question for fantasy owners who want to gamble on a second-year tight end in 2013 will really be "Fleener or Allen?" Fleener was the higher draft choice, but Allen obviously posted superior fantasy numbers. For my money, I'd take a flier on both players.

For Allen, it's certainly a concern that the top tight end from the 2012 draft class is on his team, but Fleener's presence isn't really much different from having a highly-drafted wide receiver on the team. Don't disregard Allen's 45 receptions; they're the seventh-most for any rookie tight end since 1990. And for all practical purposes, you can consider Fleener a first-round selection. That 62.5 percent hit rate looks awfully enticing.

And oh yeah, there's also that Andrew Luck guy in town.

- **The Bottom Line**

Rookie tight ends are near mirror images of first-year wide receivers; they aren't going to produce. You can acquire value by jumping on second-year tight ends who posted decent fantasy numbers during their rookie seasons.

19 How do you predict quarterback success with rookie stats?

We've learned that rookie efficiency—yards-per-carry—is the best predictor of success for second-year running backs, while bulk stats—receptions, yards, and touchdowns—are far better for wide receivers and tight ends. Moving to quarterbacks, the choice isn't as clear. Sure, yards-per-attempt is an excellent indicator of talent, but rookie quarterbacks are also very dependent on their surrounding cast. Further, we don't have the same sample size of rookie quarterbacks to study; only a handful play in a given season, compared to numerous rookie running backs and wide receivers.

I broke down the career outlooks of quarterbacks based on their rookie yards, touchdowns, and YPA.

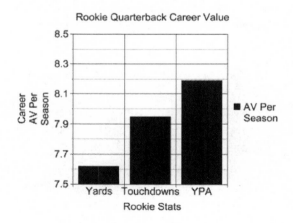

Rookie Quarterback Career Value

As was the case with running backs, efficiency trumps bulk stats for quarterbacks. That is, those rookie quarterbacks that posted high YPA have been more successful than those that have thrown for a lot of touchdowns and yards. Remember, approximate value incorporates bulk stats, but not efficiency. That means the difference between YPA—a stat that isn't a function of AV—and yards/touchdowns in terms of predicting future success is actually even greater than the numbers indicate. All other things equal, you want to draft quarterbacks who were highly efficient in their rookie seasons.

2013 Second-Year Quarterbacks

With the amazing success of Robert Griffin III, Andrew Luck, and Russell Wilson, and even the modest production from Ryan Tannehill, Nick Foles, and Brandon Weeden, 2012 has really been the year of the rookie quarterback. Let's take a look at their numbers:

- **Andrew Luck: #1 Pick, 4,374 yards, 23 TD, 7.0 YPA**
- **Robert Griffin III: #2 Pick, 3,200 yards, 20 TD, 8.1 YPA**
- **Ryan Tannehill: #8 Pick, 3,294 yards, 12 TD, 6.8 YPA**
- **Brandon Weeden: #22 Pick, 3,385 yards, 14 TD, 6.5 YPA**

- **Russell Wilson: #75 Pick, 3,118 yards, 26 TD, 7.9 YPA**
- **Nick Foles: #88 Pick, 1,699 yards, 6 TD, 6.4 YPA**

No matter how you slice it, RGIII is the cream of the rookie quarterback crop. No rookie quarterback has ever posted the type of efficiency we've seen from Griffin, and that's not even considering his amazing rushing ability. He possesses upside like we've never seen at the quarterback position, even after his knee injury. His recovery will be something to monitor closely.

Interestingly, Luck hasn't been quite as efficient as you might think. His bulk stats are great, but Luck's 7.0 YPA was barely better than that of Ryan Tannehill's 6.8 YPA in Miami. With greater efficiency and even more touchdowns, it's actually fair to wonder whether or not Russell Wilson is superior to Luck as a long-term option. Don't forget about Wilson's ability to rack up rushing yards. The primary thing Luck has going for him is his draft spot; first-round quarterbacks tend to dominate the position.

The numbers also suggest you might want to stay away from a player like Nick Foles. Even as a long-term option, Foles doesn't offer much in the way of rushing stats and his 6.4 YPA is the lowest of any rookie quarterback listed above. Further, as a third-round pick, the Eagles will have no trouble moving on from him if they need to, especially with Chip Kelly in town.

Finally, give some consideration to Redskins backup quarterback Kirk Cousins if you're in a dynasty or deep keeper league. The sample size is limited, but Cousins' 9.7 YPA is incredible. It's a gamble because of his current situation, but Cousins could be one trade away from major long-term production.

• The Bottom Line

While second-year wide receivers and tight ends are cut from the same cloth, quarterbacks in their second seasons tend to resemble running backs. That is, the ones who saw the greatest efficiency in their rookie campaign usually break out in year two. Any starting quarterback who checked in anywhere near 7.0 YPA in their first season is worthy of your consideration.

20 How much does speed matter for running backs, wide receivers, and tight ends?

The 2008 NFL Scouting Combine was one for the ages, particularly for the rookie running backs. Everyone remembers Chris Johnson's record-breaking 4.24 40-yard dash, but numerous backs were burning up the track that day in Indianapolis. All told, 13 running backs recorded sub-4.5 times, including Darren McFadden (4.33), Jamaal Charles (4.38), Rashard Mendenhall (4.41), Ray Rice (4.42), Felix Jones (4.44), Matt Forte (4.44), Steve Slaton (4.45), and Jonathan Stewart (4.46). In comparison, only four running backs checked in under 4.5 at the 2009 Combine, with the fastest time at just 4.45 (Cedric Peerman).

It's really no surprise that the 2008 rookie running back class is one of the greatest of all-time. Of the leaders in approximate value per season since 2005, nine of the top 19 came from the 2008 class. Although no one could have completely envisioned the future success of the 2008 class, there were certainly signs that the rookie backs would tear it up in the NFL.

I collected data on every running back 40-yard dash from 2005 to 2009 (giving a few years for the running backs to develop to allow for accurate assessments of their value). It's cliché to say, but for NFL running backs, speed kills.

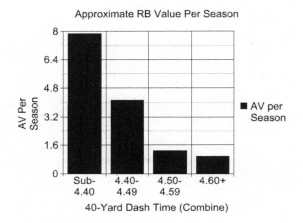

The results couldn't be more apparent; if a running back doesn't check in somewhere in the 4.4s or lower, the odds are stacked against a productive NFL career. The average value of running backs in that range is nearly four times that of backs in the 4.50 to 4.59 range. The fact that running backs who ran over 4.60 have actually performed nearly as well as those between 4.50 and 4.59 confirms that after a certain point, it's probably not worth investing in a rookie running back.

The results are particularly shocking because, from 2005 to 2009, only 31.8 percent of the running backs who ran at the Combine clocked a sub-4.5. Exactly one-third of them actually ran above 4.60. Many of those backs got drafted despite overwhelming odds against succeeding in the big leagues.

Of the 25 most successful running backs (in terms of AV per season) drafted between 2005 and 2009, the average 40-yard dash time was 4.46. Only eight of those players ran a 4.50 or worse, and only two (Shonn Greene and Frank Gore) ran worse than 4.60.

That's not to say there's some "magic" 40-yard dash time that predicts future NFL success, but it's probably accurate to claim that there's a narrow range that acts as a sort of "tipping point" (probably in the low-4.5s) for rookie running backs and, of course, faster is probably better.

That's confirmed further when you look at the "hit rate" of rookie backs; of the six backs to run sub-4.40 between 2005 and 2009, five (83.3 percent) have recorded an AV per season of at least 5.0, and the average is 7.88. Of the 38 running backs who ran between 4.40 and 4.49, only 11 (28.9 percent) have posted at least a 5.0 AV per season. Their average drops to 3.50—less than half that of the sub-4.4 backs. And of the remaining 90 backs to check in at 4.50 or greater, only six (6.7 percent) recorded an AV per season of at least 5.0. The average is just 1.14.

It's important to note that there's definitely a selection bias at work; the fastest running backs typically get drafted highest, meaning they get more opportunities to play. Nonetheless, the amazing gap between sub-4.5 runners and 4.50+ backs is substantial enough that it can't be explained solely by draft spot.

When you're examining the 2013 rookie running back class, there will be a variety of factors to consider (many of which I'll dig into deeper at a later time). If you're deciding between two different rookies, though, it's probably best to side with the speed. You could hit on a Frank Gore (4.65) once in a blue moon, but you're far more likely to find value in a Jamaal Charles (4.38) or Maurice Jones-Drew (4.39).

Further, be very critical of any running back that runs higher than a 4.50, regardless of his draft spot. Had the Cardinals been playing the percentages in the 2009 NFL Draft, they almost certainly wouldn't have wasted a pick on Beanie Wells (4.59).

- **Wide Receivers**

The success of speedy runners like Chris Johnson and Jamaal Charles isn't atypical; the majority of the league's top running backs can fly.

In the same 2008 Combine, the wide receiver class was just as fast; 20 receivers ran sub-4.5 times. Unlike the running backs, though, the receivers haven't fared too well in the big leagues. DeSean Jackson (4.35) has thus far been the best of the bunch, followed by Eddie Royal (4.39) and Pierre

Garcon (4.42). Other names who tore it up in Indianapolis that year include Dexter Jackson (4.33), Arman Shields (4.37), Will Franklin (4.37), Devin Thomas (4.40), Brandon Breazell (4.41), Keenan Burton (4.44), and James Hardy (4.45), among others.

More speed is never a bad thing, but it "matters" more at certain positions. Cornerbacks, for example, need to have the recovery speed to catch up to receivers, so it's rare to see any successful cornerback run above a 4.50. We saw the same phenomenon with running backs, which was a bit unexpected. When we analyze wide receivers, the fastest ones have understandably had more success than others, but perhaps not to the degree you'd expect.

I've sorted both running backs and wide receivers based on their approximate value per season and their 40-yard dash times at the Combine. I used every player from 2005 to 2009 (345 total) to allow time for each to develop in the NFL.

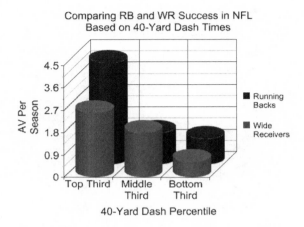

Comparing RB and WR Success in NFL
Based on 40-Yard Dash Times

Speed obviously wins out for both groups, but the drop in NFL production from the running backs ranked in the top third to those ranked in the middle third (34th to 67th percentile) is extraordinary. On average, running backs who ranked in the top third of all 40-yard dash times have been over three times as valuable in terms of approximate value as those who with moderate speed. On the flip side, the fastest wide receivers have barely outperformed players with moderate speed (between 4.45 and 4.54).

Since there's such a steep drop between the fastest running backs and those with a modest amount of speed, there's not much of a difference between the middle tier of backs and those ranked in the bottom third. That's pretty straightforward; if the chances of NFL success are already minimal for backs who clock between, say, 4.55 and 4.60, they aren't going to be too much worse for the slowest runners.

Since wide receivers with moderate speed can and have produced big-time numbers in the NFL, the drop between them and the slowest players at their position is steep—much more so than for running backs. In effect, the "cutoff" point of NFL success for wide receivers is simply lower than it is for running backs.

One of the reasons we see receivers with moderate speed have success in the NFL is that size probably matters more for them than for running backs. As the NFL has become more and more pass-heavy, backs like Johnson and Charles have been able to thrive despite small frames.

Meanwhile, take a look at the top 10 wide receivers in fantasy football in 2012 (standard scoring): Calvin Johnson, Brandon Marshall, Dez Bryant, A.J. Green, Demaryius Thomas, Vincent Jackson, Andre Johnson, Eric Decker, Julio Jones, and Roddy White. Every single one of those players stands at least 6-1 and weighs a minimum of 201 pounds. The *average* (the average!) is 6-3 and 220 pounds. Some of them ran outstanding 40-yard dashes, but others (Marshall, Bryant, Jackson, Decker, White) didn't light it up.

Thus, it isn't that being fast doesn't help receivers, but rather that the speed "cutoff" isn't as stringent as it is for running backs. Receivers also need two things to maximize their chances of success in the NFL. The first is size (especially height). The second is at least a moderate amount of speed (ideally under 4.55). A bunch of big receivers with moderate speed have succeeded of late—Marshall (4.52), Kenny Britt (4.51), Jordy Nelson (4.51), Dwayne Bowe (4.51), Hakeem Nicks (4.50)—but they're all very large. Meanwhile, only one receiver drafted between 2005 and 2009 has recorded a respectable AV per season (above 5.0) after running worse than a 4.52 at the Combine.

That player is Davone Bess, and he's hardly dominating fantasy football.

- **Tight Ends**

In hindsight, it's pretty easy to see why Jimmy Graham has become one of the dominant tight ends in the NFL: a 6-7, 265-pound frame, a 38.5-inch vertical, and 4.53 speed. Graham is a bit of a freak, but he's not the only athlete-turned-tight end who has succeeded in the NFL.

Tight ends are used to cause matchup problems for defenses, and one of the ways the best receiving tight ends get open because is by outrunning linebackers. However, tight ends are unique in that they're often asked to utilize different aspects of their game based on various factors, such as the play-call or the defensive personnel. Tight ends must be versatile; in addition to beating linebackers with speed, they need to be strong enough to block and big enough to outmuscle defensive backs in the passing game.

That's displayed in the different types of tight ends out there; speedsters like Graham, Greg Olsen (4.50), and Dustin Keller (4.53) primarily use speed to work defenders. Others, such as Rob Gronkowski (4.75), Brandon Pettigrew (4.83) and Jermichel Finley (4.82), use size and position.

For both running backs and wide receivers, there's a cutoff point after which players probably won't succeed in the NFL (around 4.50 for running backs and 4.55 for wide receivers). There are exceptions, but for the most part you won't see too many successful running backs or wide receivers running 4.65 40-yard dashes.

For tight ends, however, there doesn't seem to be such a distinct cutoff. On the next page, you can see many of the league's "slow" tight ends have still produced.

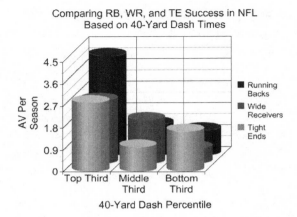

Comparing RB, WR, and TE Success in NFL
Based on 40-Yard Dash Times

The total production for tight ends drafted from 2005 to 2009 who ranked in the bottom third in 40 time is greater than that for running backs or wide receivers. Actually, slower tight ends (4.80-plus) have posted *superior numbers* than tight ends with moderate speed (4.72 to 4.79). That's probably due to randomness or a small sample size—I used 79 total tight ends—but it's still evidence that slower players can succeed at tight end more so than at other positions.

That's not to say that speed is a bad thing; more speed is always better. The dropoff from the fastest tight ends (4.71 or better) to the second tier is still pretty substantial. Since 2005, some of the tight ends to fall in this upper echelon include Vernon Davis, Aaron Hernandez, Owen Daniels, Fred Davis, and Jared Cook.

When looking at tight ends coming out of the draft (or even veterans), speed should be a factor, but not to the same degree as for running backs, or even wide receivers. Unlike the latter two positions, you can't really eliminate any tight ends due solely to their 40-yard dash time. Zach Miller has been a capable NFL tight end despite running a 4.87, for example.

If a tight end is small in stature, however, he better run extremely well; sub-4.65 is optimal. If he doesn't have top speed, he should make up for it in size and strength.

- **The Bottom Line**

The idea that sub 4.50 running backs have the odds stacked against them can be used when analyzing all types of running backs. The most obvious application is to rookies, but you can use historic Combine 40 times to predict success for other backs as well. If a slower running back has a track history of NFL production, the number probably doesn't matter as much. But for second and third-year backs who managed to produce early in their careers, a lack of ideal speed could indicate trouble down the road. I'm looking at you Alfred Morris.

When you're searching for the next elite wide receiver, whether he's a rookie or a third-year man, emphasize height and weight. The best receivers are at least 6-1, enhancing their chances of scoring in the red zone. Unlike running backs, 4.55 wide receivers can and do thrive in the NFL.

Finally, speed really isn't too much of a concern for tight ends. However, if a tight end doesn't have elite speed, he better have good size. A 6-2, 250-pound tight end who runs a 4.89 probably isn't going to cut it.

21 How much does quarterback height affect NFL performance?

In the 2001 NFL Draft, the Falcons traded up to draft Virginia Tech quarterback Michael Vick. At only 6-1, the Falcons were hoping Vick's rocket arm and blazing speed could make up for his short stature. Later in the same draft, the Chargers hit it big (although they never realized it) on Drew Brees. Standing at the same height as Vick, Brees has relied on pinpoint accuracy to overcome being one of the shortest players at his position drafted in the last decade.

In studying predictors of NFL success at the quarterback position, I decided to move away from studying speed—as I did for running backs, wide receivers, and tight ends—because only recently has the NFL transitioned to a league in which mobile quarterbacks can be true difference-makers. Even during Vick's glory days in Atlanta, he was one of just a handful of passers to rely on his speed to make plays. With the NFL's adoption of the read-option and similar offensive styles, however, quarterback speed is now playing a major role in success at the position.

I charted the height of every quarterback (as measured at the Combine) drafted in the first two rounds since 2000. I analyzed only highly-drafted quarterbacks to make sure all of the subjects were on a relatively even playing field. For the few quarterbacks who didn't start in their first NFL season, I disregarded every season up until their first start.

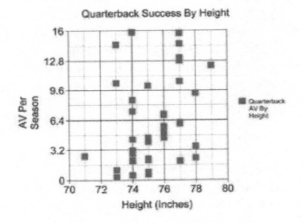

The quarterbacks are pretty scattered, although there does appear to be a slight correlation between height and success. Interestingly, four of the six most successful first or second-round quarterbacks drafted since 2000—Philip Rivers, Matt Ryan, Ben Roethlisberger, and Eli Manning—all checked in at exactly 77 inches.

If we break down the result into group averages, the results become slightly clearer.

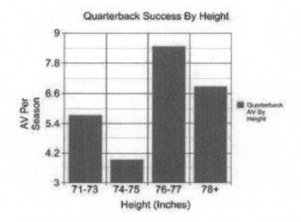

You see some success in the 71 to 73-inch group, but that's probably the result of a small sample size. Only five such quarterbacks were drafted in the first or second round between 2000 and 2010, and two of them were Vick and Brees. The fact that the AV-per-season drops for quarterbacks in the 74 to 75-inch group suggests the success of the shorter quarterbacks is a fluke. The success of the passers who stand 76 and 77 inches tall, on the other hand, is pretty remarkable.

Perhaps the best evidence that there's at least a small correlation between height and NFL production is the success rates for each group. Of the quarterbacks in this study who were measured between 71 and 75 inches, only 26.0 percent have posted at least 5.0 AV per season. Meanwhile, nearly three times as many quarterbacks who stand at least

76 inches tall—70.1 percent—have reached that mark.

• Correlation versus Causation

Soon after being named as the head coach of the Philadelphia Eagles, Chip Kelly mentioned that he doesn't necessarily care too much about quarterback height, but rather about hand size. Quarterbacks need to be able to control the football with ease, and big hands obviously allow for that.

That got me to thinking: could the success we see from tall quarterbacks not really be because they're tall, but because tall quarterbacks typically have bigger hands? A short quarterback with a larger-than-average hand size would then be predicted to have as much success as a taller quarterback with the same hand size, regardless of their difference in height. There's not enough trustworthy data out there on hand size, but it's something to consider as a potential explanation for the height/success correlation at the quarterback position.

• The Bottom Line

Quarterback height is correlated with NFL success. Will the trend continue in the future? The rise of mobile quarterbacks could decrease the need for 6-4 height, but it's tough to say right now. As of 2013, use height as a tiebreaker for two equally-rated quarterbacks.

22 Do injuries offer potential value?

There's no doubt that 2012 was the year of the comeback player in the NFL. After suffering major knee injuries in 2011, running backs Jamaal Charles and Adrian Peterson combined for over 3,600 rushing yards and 19 total touchdowns. "All Day" Peterson's 2,000-yard performance was so sensational that it has many pondering the limits of the human body. And how could we forget about the Comeback Player of the Year—Mr. Peyton Manning? Even his biggest supporters couldn't have envisioned a 4,659-yard, 37-touchdown season.

For every big-name comeback story, however, there was a disappointment as well. Darren McFadden, DeMarco Murray, and Fred Jackson were all unable to overcome their injury demons; all of them finished at least 19 spots below their preseason ADP.

Prior to the season, McFadden and Murray were actually both players I targeted. I got lucky that neither player ended up on more than one of my teams, but the truth is that I thought their injuries in the prior season were causing owners to drop them too far in the rankings. In short, I figured those injuries actually provided value to McFadden, Murray, and a handful of other players. While it's not inherently optimal to choose a player with a recent injury over a healthy one, I figured the difference between ADP and true value was greatest for injured players, i.e. owners inflate the importance of a low-frequency event and subsequently downgrade players coming off of injuries more than they deserve.

Guess what? I was wrong. I recently studied the biggest injuries to skill position players that occurred between 2008 and 2011. Some of the names on the list are Tom Brady, Steve Smith, Rashard Mendenhall, Knowshon Moreno, Wes Welker, and of course the players listed above. I charted their preseason ADP in the year following their season-ending injury, along with their final season rank at their position.

Overall, I examined the 38 highest-ranked players coming off of a recent injury—not a huge sample size but perhaps enough for the dramatic results to be significant. Of those 38 players, only 12 improved upon their preseason ADP. The average drop was nine spots in the rankings.

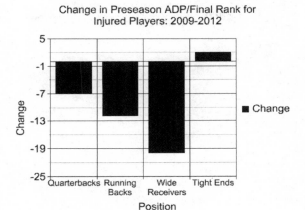

Change in Preseason ADP/Final Rank for Injured Players: 2009-2012

Quarterbacks, running backs, and wide receivers all dropped between seven and 20 spots from their preseason ADP. Those results are so major that it makes up for the small sample. It's unclear if tight ends are really capable of coming back from injuries better than players at other positions—tight ends actually rose an average of two spots from their ADP—but it's worth noting that there were just four highly-ranked tight ends who suffered season-ending injuries over the time period studied, and only one of them (Brandon Pettigrew in 2010) rose significantly.

Even if we confine the results to only those players who were ranked as a No. 1 or 2 option at their position before the year, the results don't improve. For those elite players, the average drop is 13 spots.

Ultimately, it doesn't appear as though players coming off of major injuries offer much value as a whole. While it might be tempting to take the stud running back coming off of a torn ACL or the speedy wide receiver who broke his leg last year because they begin to drop in your draft, remember that there are more seasons that resemble McFadden's 2012 than Peterson's.

- **The Bottom Line**

You don't need to purposely avoid all players coming off injuries, because some of them might still hold value. Still, you better be damn sure that the 27-year old running back coming off of an ACL tear has really dropped enough in the rankings to offer superior value to the 24-year old back off of his first 1,000-yard season.

23 Can early-season average draft position (ADP) be useful in August?

There aren't many tools in the fantasy owner's arsenal more valuable than Average Draft Position (ADP). Mock drafts are fun, but they can actually be harmful to owners. In any draft, certain players have a range in which they could potentially get drafted based on how the draft unfolds. Fantasy football drafts often create a butterfly effect of sorts; change a single selection or replace just one owner and the results of any particular draft can be drastically altered.

When you participate in or view a mock draft, the majority of players will be selected comfortably within their "range of possible outcomes," i.e. they'll be at or near their "average" spot. Some players, however, will be in outlying positions near the high or low end of their pre-draft range. If you participate in a draft in which Aaron Rodgers drops into the third round, for example, you'll likely be an unhappy owner if you expect to wait to grab Rodgers in the same round of your next draft.

Because of that, ADP is the most useful way to determine players' value. In effect, ADP limits the randomness of individual drafts to provide you with an accurate depiction of reality. If you see that LeSean McCoy's current ADP is No. 13 overall, you can expect that, in most drafts, McCoy will get selected anywhere from the late-first to the mid-second.

- **Using ADP to Judge Rankings**

I'm a big believer in creating your own projections and rankings. You can and should collect as much data as possible from as many legitimate sources as you can, but at the end of the day, your rankings should be drafted independently of public opinion.

However, that doesn't mean you shouldn't consider the views of others. *After* you make your initial rankings, it can be helpful to view ADP to learn where you stand in relation to others. In no way should your original rankings simply mirror public opinion, but when you have a player ranked wildly differently than the masses, he's worth a second look.

The reason for this is a phenomenon known as "wisdom of the crowds" whereby the aggregate of expert opinions is often superior to the majority of those individual opinions taken in isolation. If you bet on football games using the consensus picks from professional sports bettors, for example, the results are typically superior to those from most of the bettors themselves.

Of course, ADP in late-August is hardly a collection of expert opinions. By that time, you've had just about every type of owner participate in drafts and there's a whole lot of "groupthink" that has taken place. In many cases, a previously quality expert opinion on a sleeper may have catapulted him so far up boards that he no longer offers value. Similarly, some players fly under the radar simply because they haven't received a ton of publicity.

In the beginning of the year, however, there aren't many first-year fantasy owners participating in drafts. Instead, it's more advanced players who are fresh off of the 2012 season. Without consensus rankings published yet, they're working off of their own research and analysis. Most important, they typically haven't let the opinions of others cloud their own judgments.

Thus, looking at early-season ADP can give us a really strong indication of market value for the upcoming season. Below, I've pasted the standard scoring ADP for the top 30 players, as of February 2013.

1. RB Adrian Peterson
2. RB Arian Foster
3. RB Doug Martin
4. RB Ray Rice
5. WR Calvin Johnson
6. RB Marshawn Lynch
7. RB Trent Richardson
8. RB C.J. Spiller
9. QB Aaron Rodgers
10. RB Jamaal Charles
11. QB Drew Brees

12. WR Demaryius Thomas
13. RB LeSean McCoy
14. QB Tom Brady
15. WR A.J. Green
16. RB Alfred Morris
17. WR Brandon Marshall
18. TE Rob Gronkowski
19. WR Dez Bryant
20. WR Julio Jones
21. RB Matt Forte
22. TE Jimmy Graham
23. QB Peyton Manning
24. WR Percy Harvin
25. WR Victor Cruz
26. RB Chris Johnson
27. QB Cam Newton
28. RB Stevan Ridley
29. RB David Wilson
30. RB Darren McFadden

- ## Using Early-Season ADP in August

It would obviously be unwise to blindly use early-season ADP when you draft. Your board can and should change quite a bit leading up to your draft. However, it's still valuable to understand the opinions of the most advanced owners out there, and early-season ADP can allow for that.

The most useful way to use the above numbers, perhaps, is to seek players who have dropped without much reason to fall. If Drew Brees falls from his current No. 11 draft slot because he hurt his elbow in the preseason, for example, you may or may not find value at his new draft slot. You have to adjust for any and all new information.

However, if Alfred Morris falls from being the 10th overall running back selected in the middle of the second round to the 13th running back in the back of the third and you can't uncover any reason to explain the decline, chances are it was because the advanced owners have a higher opinion of Morris than the general public. If that coincides with your own projections for Morris, you can rest easier knowing you might have found true value.

- **The Bottom Line**

If you get a chance, take a look at early ADP in February or March, and tuck it away. It could very well give you an idea of which players the advanced owners like when you pull it back out in August, and that information is useful.

24 How can you tell which players are safe and which are risky?

In fall of 2012 (and 2008, to a lesser degree), Nate Silver gained notoriety for accurately forecasting the presidential election; Silver correctly predicted the winner of all 50 states (after missing just one in 2008). Before recently, Silver was known primarily as the creator of PECOTA—a system he created to project the performance of baseball players.

PECOTA, which stands for Player Empirical Comparison and Optimization Test Algorithm (naturally), forecasts player performance by assigning players with "comparables"—other players whose past performance and characteristics closely resemble those of the player in question. PECOTA assigns similarity scores to a player's comparables and then projects future performance based on how similar players in analogous situations performed in the past.

PECOTA has widely been recognized as one of the most innovative (and accurate) sports projection models ever created. Perhaps the coolest aspect of PECOTA is that it provides a range of outcomes for each player; instead of saying "okay, Player A is going to hit .300 this year," it says "based on similar players in the past, Player A is pretty likely to hit around .300, but he could also hit .250 if things go awry, or even .350 if everything goes his way. That might sound wishy-washy, but PECOTA really captures the uncertainty involved with forecasting.

That uncertainty can be harnessed for good. By analyzing the range of potential outcomes for a player based on his comparables, we can get a really good sense of how well or poorly his season might turn out. We can also measure his upside and his risk, among other things.

- ## Similarity Scores in Football

Luckily for all of us, similarity scores have made their way into football. At rotoViz, you can use custom similarity score apps for your projections. You specify the player you want to analyze, and the apps provide 20 comparables—the most similar players in terms of past stats and other criteria, such as age, height, and weight. Frank DuPont, the founder of rotoViz, explains it best:

> *Similarity based projections are probably the most powerful thing that I use to draft my fantasy team that most fantasy owners just don't have at their fingertips. Similarity based projections address shortfalls in other projection systems that might have a tough time accounting for variables that aren't linear (age for instance) or perhaps variables that might interact with each other (like receiver size and touchdown totals). Instead of saying that a receiving*

yard is worth 0.7 receiving yards when projecting the following season's fantasy results, as a regression formula might tell you, I just look at how a group of similar players performed and make an assumption that my subject player might fit within the range of how similar receivers performed.

Similarity scores will do generally a good job of capturing the way that variables might interact. A variable like total carries could have a different impact on a running back depending on that back's age or size. Similarity scores recognize the difficulty of forecasting with a bunch of variables that might not be linear and might interact with each other, making the simple assumption that if you look at a similar group, the results will be similar. If you take the time to backtest this assumption, you'll find that similarity scores do improve on the predictive ability of a simple linear regression.

One sort of pre-emptive note is that similarity scores are going to have a very difficult time addressing extreme outliers. Similarity scores use the past to forecast the future, so when a reasonable approximation can't be found in the past, it's going to go to the next closest thing, which might not be that close.

By using similarity scores and generating comparables for players we want to analyze, we can gain all sorts of unique insights that wouldn't otherwise be available. In the sections below, I've used the similarity apps at rotoViz to project the ceilings and floors (upside and downside) for the elite players at each position. It's obviously vital to hit on the first few picks in your draft—if you find studs in the first four rounds, you can pretty much "bullshit" your way to a championship with sound waiver wire additions.

Anyway, when we're searching for value in the early rounds, it's often advantageous to value safety, i.e. players with high floors. In an area of the draft where the cost is high and every player possesses great upside, owners have the most to gain, ironically, by minimizing their losses. In most cases, the players with the highest floors are those with the greatest projected points within the bottom tier of their similar players. In effect, we're asking "what's the worst this guy could do?"

I'll use the similarity score apps to make a case for one elite player at each position.

- **Quarterbacks**

If you participate in a 12-team fantasy football league in which every owner is evenly matched, you'll have an 8.3 percent chance to win the championship, i.e. you're an underdog from the start. Because of the nature of fantasy football, it's typically best to implement a high-risk draft strategy. By seeking high-risk, high-reward players, you'll maximize your chances of long-term success.

Having said that, I typically advocate utilizing a low-variance strategy early in drafts—the first round or two—emphasizing safety over upside. Every player has a high ceiling in the initial portion of drafts, meaning you have the most to gain by maximizing the floors of your selections. That's the primary impetus behind the popularity of drafting elite quarterbacks; Aaron Rodgers, Drew Brees & Co. have value in being so reliable from season to season.

Of course, you can't seek consistency at all costs. Every draft pick comes with at the price of forgoing other selections, and drafting a quarterback early could leave you bare at other positions. Further, quarterback is a relatively deep position—you can find a Matthew Stafford, Tony Romo, or Matt Ryan in the middle rounds—whereas potentially elite running backs are much scarcer. The cost of obtaining the consistency of a player like Rodgers is passing on the scarcity of a running back like Doug Martin.

It sure would be nice if there were an elite quarterback who didn't cost a first-round pick. One who has a track record of big-time fantasy success. One with three play-makers at wide receiver and a talented defense to get him the ball. One with both the safety and upside of his more highly-coveted counterparts.

Oh, now wait. There's a quarterback just like that getting drafted in the back of the second round (or even as late as the fourth in some PPR leagues), and his name is Peyton Manning. Surprised? So was I.

Using the custom QB Similarity Scores App, I calculated the upside and downside for the draft's top four quarterbacks—Rodgers, Brees, Brady, and Manning—by charting the fantasy points scored by their top four and bottom four comparables, respectively, in each statistical category (minimum of six games played).

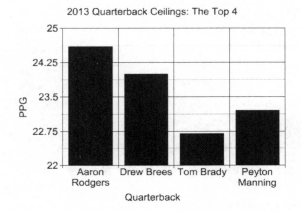

In terms of upside, the quarterbacks are all grouped together pretty tightly. Rodgers has the advantage because of his rushing ability and age, while Brees is right behind him since he could very well become the first quarterback to throw 6,000 passes in one season. For the most part, though, there's not a massive difference here. Now let's take a look at the players' floors. . .

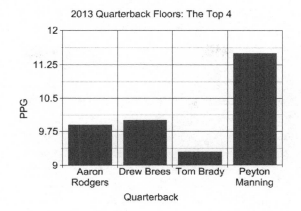

Manning's bottom four comparables in each category have generated a floor that's nearly two fantasy points per game higher than the comparables for Rodgers, Brees, and Brady. You could argue that Manning has the best offensive weapons of the bunch, and he posted 4,659 yards and 37 touchdowns in his first year in Denver. There's even more upside to be had as Manning's comfort level with his teammates and new town grows.

Now let's talk about the obvious perils. It's not like one season of solid play completely erases all risks that Manning assumed entering the 2012 season. He's still pretty fresh off of four neck surgeries, and at 37 years old, Manning is right on the edge of the historic quarterback production cliff.

As it is with any player, the question is if the risks outweigh the rewards. As I mentioned earlier, the risk is a late-second round pick—significantly better than the mid-first to early-second you'd have to spend on Rodgers, Brees, or Brady. Actually, Manning's current ADP is at least eight spots behind each of the other three passers. Nonetheless, I'd argue Manning is nearly as safe as the trio.

To get a decent sense of the risk/reward surrounding each player, I added the ceiling and floor production—the average points per game for the top four comparables plus the average for the bottom four comparables in each statistical category.

1. **Peyton Manning: 34.7**
2. **Aaron Rodgers: 34.5**
3. **Drew Brees: 34.0**
4. **Tom Brady: 32.0**

Pretty good for a player getting selected just a few spots ahead of Robert Griffin III. It's also worth noting that Manning was the only quarterback of the four that had all of his comparables play in the majority of games. While the average games played for the comparables of Rodgers, Brees, and Brady was between 13.7 and 13.9, Manning's comparables participated in 15.2 games per season.

Ultimately, I think the QB Similarity Scores App paints a pretty picture for the veteran quarterback.

There are of course concerns, but even considering Manning's age and potential neck problems, his floor is at least similar to "The Big Three" first-round quarterbacks. If that's the case, he's quality value at his 20th overall ADP.

Further, if you can draft Manning in the back of the second round, you won't have to worry as much about missing out on running back scarcity. With an elite runner in the first round and another top back in the third, you could legitimately be looking at a core of Arian Foster/Doug Martin, Peyton Manning, and Stevan Ridley/Matt Forte.

If Manning is able to make it through another 16-game season in 2013, you could potentially have your consistency cake and it eat it too.

- ## Running Backs

A lot of fantasy football articles are written for shock value; they often have attention-grabbing titles and make outrageous claims for the sole purpose of getting clicks.

This isn't one of them.

Tampa Bay Bucs running back Doug Martin truly deserves consideration as the top overall player on your board in 2013. Here's why.

In 2012, Martin finished second among all running backs in fantasy points in both standard and PPR leagues. The rookie burst onto the scene with over 1,900 total yards, 49 receptions, and 12 total touchdowns.

As it stands right now, Martin is getting selected as the fifth running back off of the board in early drafts; his No. 5 overall ADP puts him behind Adrian Peterson, Arian Foster, Ray Rice, and Marshawn Lynch, in that order.

Since you'll need to use an early first-round pick on Martin to acquire his services, your focus should be on how safe he is, i.e. how likely he is to be a bust in 2013. To determine the ceilings and floors for the draft's elite running backs, I used the RB Similarity Score app. Since the similarity apps provide a range of potential outcomes for the upcoming season, they can address the uncertainty built into forecasting any given player.

It's true that the similarity apps could have trouble projecting players coming off of outlying seasons; since there aren't too many seasons like Peterson's 2012 year, for example, the regression we see in his comps might be slightly overblown. Having said that, I think there's still a lot of value in assessing the extremes of the comps—the top and bottom 20 percent. The majority of evenly-priced players will have very similar projected points. In analyzing the extremes, though, we can get a sense of the deviation for historical comps, i.e. what's the upside and the downside for any particular player?

I charted the ceilings for the top six backs in terms of current ADP—the five listed above and Trent Richardson.

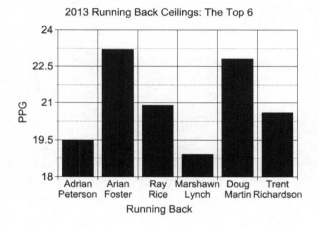

Note that the chart ranges from 18 to 24 PPG, so the expected production for the top six backs is similar. Again, Peterson's ceiling is likely higher than what's listed here, but it's still interesting to see how the backs' upside coincides with age. I don't think it's any coincidence that Lynch, coming off of a season with very similar numbers to Martin, possesses the lowest ceiling of the bunch heading into his age 27 season. In terms of upside alone, you have to wonder why Lynch is getting drafted ahead of Martin or Richardson.

That question intensifies when we examine the floors for the backs.

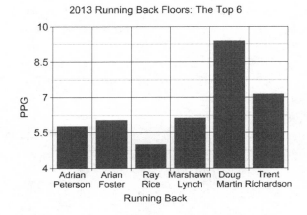

Here, the value of the young backs shines. Despite rushing for only 950 yards at 3.56 YPC in his rookie season, Richardson joins Martin as having the "safest" historical comps. That's not surprising when you consider that running backs typically peak in efficiency right when they come into the league, and it's a gradual decline from there. When you have young backs at the peak of their games and you put them in high-volume situations without much competition—as is the case with both Martin and Richardson—you have the makings of low-risk/high-reward players.

That idea is confirmed when we look at the plots for year-to-year change in fantasy points for the comparables of Martin and Lynch (contained within the similarity apps).

Doug Martin Plot

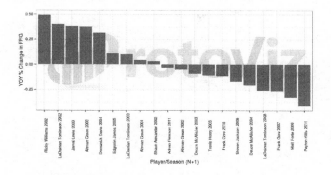

Marshawn Lynch Plot

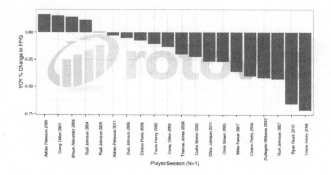

The novelty of rotoViz is allowing for superior data visualization. There's no better way to visualize the possible 2013 seasons for Martin and Lynch than the plots above. Could Lynch outperform Martin in 2013? Sure, but it's not likely.

Think about this. Martin has five comps who posted a +25% change in fantasy points per game. Lynch has zero. Lynch has eight comps who recorded a -25% change in PPG and two that cut their PPG in half. Martin has four and zero, respectively. If that's not evidence that Martin has a dramatically higher ceiling *and* floor than Lynch, I don't know what is.

- **Games Played**

While the number of games played by the backs' comps is susceptible to randomness, it's still interesting to see that the projected health for Rice, Martin, and Richardson—the three youngest backs examined here—is remarkably better than that for Foster, Peterson, and Lynch (particularly the latter two). Take a look at the average games played for the runners' four worst comps:

- **Peterson: 4.8**
- **Foster: 8.8**
- **Rice: 10.3**
- **Lynch: 5.8**
- **Martin: 11.8**
- **Richardson: 10.0**

The numbers are representative of each player's probability of staying on the field in 2013. As you'd imagine, younger is better.

Martin is a young back at the peak of his game. Likely to see 350-plus touches in 2013, Martin is a good bet to again beat out fellow second-year back Richardson in terms of YPC. Martin's ceiling is the second-highest of the top six backs—behind only Foster—and his floor is the greatest by a wide margin. The floor for Martin's comps is actually nearly double that for those of Rice.

In terms of the top overall pick, Martin's name should be in there with Peterson and Foster. The Texans running back will be 27 when the 2013 season begins. It's difficult to uncover seasons similar to Peterson's 2012, but he's about to turn 28. Although AP caught 40 passes last year, he's not the same threat as Martin out of the backfield, and pass-catching backs have historically proven to be safer options at the position.

Martin is by no means the surefire top player on the board, but to dismiss him out of hand would be a mistake.

- **Wide Receivers**

The distinguishing feature of the similarity score apps—the trait that gives them an advantage over traditional projections—is that they provide a range of potential outcomes for any given player. There's a certain level of uncertainty in any prediction, and the apps account for that.

When implementing uncertainty into projections, the hurdle many fail to overcome is establishing a definitive prediction at all. It can be tempting to examine a player's spectrum of potential outcomes and say, "Well, this guy could score 22 points per game, or he could score 11, but he'll probably be somewhere in between. And this player might score 20 points per game, or he could score 9 points per game, but he'll also probably be somewhere in between. So what the hell do I do?"

The most obvious solution is to generate an average for each player based on their comparables. That certainly has its advantages; taking the mean production of 20 very similar players will generally give you a quality projection.

However, doing that ignores a feature of the similarity scores that really makes them so useful— the magnitude of their range of outcomes. A player whose floor is 10 points and whose ceiling is 20 points could very well have the same mean projection as a player with a 13-point floor and 17-point ceiling. But there's a difference between the two, and it needs to be captured.

I charted the ceilings for the top half-dozen wide receivers in terms of current ADP—the only six who are getting selected in the first two rounds. These are the ceiling projections for each player based on their top four comparables in each statistical category for PPR leagues—receptions, yards, and touchdowns. I threw out any comps who didn't participate in at least six games.

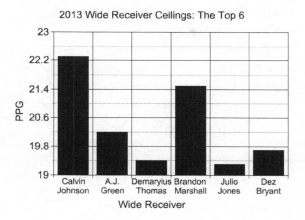

It's not too surprising to see Calvin Johnson with the highest projected ceiling. In reality, his ceiling is probably even higher than listed because it's difficult to find comps for a player coming off of a 122/1,964/5 season.

While A.J. Green, Demaryius Thomas, Julio Jones, and Dez Bryant all possess similar upside, it's interesting to see Brandon Marshall towering above them with a ceiling of 21.5 points per game. Marshall's 118 receptions in 2012 don't hurt, but he'd still be the clear No. 2 if his peak receptions per game—currently at 6.69—were closer to the average of the group (which is barely less at 6.57).

Marshall's ceiling as a highly-targeted No. 1 option with Jay Cutler at quarterback is probably higher than that for Thomas and Jones, at least, simply because they have to share looks with other talented receivers. Jones in particular probably doesn't have the sort of upside everyone who is drafting him in the middle of the second round is expecting. Unless the Falcons completely shift their game plan to emphasize Jones over Roddy White *and* defenses tailor their schemes to allow Jones to see more single-coverage, he might not have top three potential.

Since all of these receivers are currently getting selected in the first two rounds, it might be more valuable to examine their floors. The easiest way to acquire value in the first few rounds is to minimize risk; everyone has awesome upside, so it's just as easy to hit a home run by simply trying to make contact as it is by swinging for the fences.

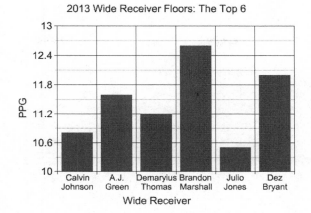

2013 Wide Receiver Floors: The Top 6

Quite surprisingly, Marshall has a higher floor than each of the other top-rated receivers. Again, Johnson's numbers are deflated due to a lack of truly similar comps. You could say he'll see increased defensive attention coming off of one of the premiere seasons in NFL history, but how much more coverage could he really see?

To get a decent sense of the risk/reward surrounding each player, I added the ceiling and floor production—the average points per game for the top four comparables plus the average for the bottom four comparables in each statistical category.

1. **Brandon Marshall: 34.1**
2. **Calvin Johnson: 33.1**
3. **A.J. Green: 31.8**

4. Dez Bryant: 31.7
5. Demaryius Thomas: 30.6
6. Julio Jones: 29.8

There seems to be a bigger difference between Marshall and Jones than their respective ADPs (2.02 for Marshall and 2.05 for Jones) suggest. Although Jones is entering the sought-after third year of his career, wide receivers at his age have still historically produced slightly worse numbers than those at Marshall's. Plus, their ages are already factored into their comps. I wouldn't specifically target Marshall in a dynasty league, but for 2013 alone, there's probably only one receiver in fantasy football who should be rated higher.

- **Tight Ends**

Aaron Hernandez is a short (6-1) tight end who has never played 16 games in a year, doesn't have a 1,000-yard season to his name, and plays as the No. 2 tight end on his own team. But he's still getting selected in the third round of fantasy drafts as the third tight end off of the board. Why?

In my opinion, Hernandez has a limited ceiling, even in the Patriots' potent offense. Although fellow tight end Rob Gronkowski obviously doesn't *completely* prevent Hernandez from lighting it up, having a Pro Bowl tight end as the first option over the middle of the field is still a drain on Hernandez's fantasy upside. Unless Gronkowski gets hurt, I don't think Hernandez can *really* break out.

But who really cares about my opinion? You should really just concern yourself with what the numbers say regarding Hernandez in 2013. In regards to his ceiling and floor, the Tight End Similarity Score app has a lot to say.

At the tight end position, two players—Gronkowski and Jimmy Graham—stand out above the rest with current ADPs of 1.11 and 2.03, respectively. A tier below, Hernandez checks in at third at 3.08, and Jason Witten is getting drafted fourth at 4.02.

I graphed the potential upside for those top four tight ends based on their top comps. I used PPR scoring.

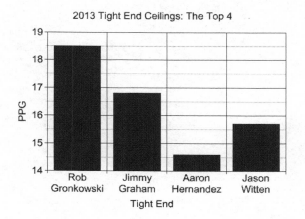

Not surprisingly, Gronkowski and Graham lead the pack. Gronkowski's upside in particular is outstanding, as his peak season is 1.7 points per game higher than Graham's. More important, the numbers seem to confirm my suspicion that Hernandez isn't necessarily a high-upside player. His top comps have posted 1.1 points per game lower than Witten—a soon-to-be 31-year old.

Worse, Hernandez doesn't possess a very high floor, either, i.e. he's not really a safe pick.

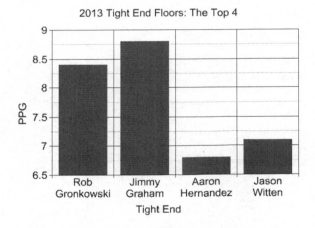

2013 Tight End Floors: The Top 4

Again, Hernandez checks in below Witten. The production of his bottom four comps is just 77 percent of that for Graham's comps. Adding the ceiling and floor production numbers together, we can get a good idea of the risk/reward surrounding each tight end.

1. Rob Gronkowski: 26.9
2. Jimmy Graham: 25.6
3. Jason Witten: 22.8
4. Aaron Hernandez: 21.4

No matter how you slice it, Hernandez simply isn't worth his current third-round ADP. He has just a miniscule probability of going for 1,200/10, and there's good evidence that he shouldn't even get drafted ahead of Witten in PPR leagues.

- ## The Bottom Line

When it comes to drafting, it's really important to understand risk and reward. You generally want to minimize downside early in the draft by selecting safe players and maximize upside later with high-ceiling options. But how do you calculate true risk and reward?

One way is to generate "comparables" for each player using similarity scores. By looking at how players with similar traits performed in similar situations in the past, you can gain a really solid understanding of the range of potential outcomes for a given player. In doing that, it becomes easier to make ceiling and floor projections in order to identify true risk and reward.

Comparables are useful because the uncertainty that is inherent to any projection is built into the system. By incorporating that uncertainty into your rankings, you can make more accurate predictions. I gave you examples of how to use similarity scores for the elite players at each position, and you can check out the comparables for any player at rotoViz.

25 When and how should you draft a defense?

Fantasy owners sure have wised up over the years. Back when I began playing fantasy football about a decade ago, the top defenses from the previous season would fly off of the board in the middle rounds (sometimes before we even got into the double-digits). And I'm not talking about the leagues with my Uncle Bruce; I'm talking "expert" leagues.

Nowadays, defenses are rarely chosen before the last few rounds of fantasy drafts. Owners have realized that the success of NFL defenses is simply too fluky to count on. The most consistent defensive stat—points allowed—still has a year-to-year correlation of just 0.35. That basically means that only 35 percent of the points a defense allows "carry over" to the subsequent season, with the other 65 percent regressing toward a league mean.

Plus, the majority of defensive fantasy points come from things like interceptions, fumble recoveries, and touchdowns, not points yielded. All of those stats are extremely volatile. Good luck trying to predict which team will lead the league in fumble recoveries and defensive touchdowns this year. It ain't happening.

On top of all of that, the scarcity of defenses is minimal. Whereas the elite quarterbacks and running backs are projected to score dozens of points more than their second-tier counterparts, the lack of consistency among team defenses means projecting one to score many more points than another isn't a wise decision.

Of course, there is a little bit of predictability among defenses. Even if it is minimal, a small advantage is superior to none at all. Even though points allowed is the most consistent stat among defenses, it isn't extremely useful to fantasy owners because fantasy points are often rewarded on a tiered basis; that is, owners get a specific number of points for a shutout, a slightly lower number of points if their defense allows 2-7 points, and so on. This tiered system creates more volatility for fantasy owners, and thus decreases the value of its practical application into projections.

Instead, I suggest fantasy owners choose their defense based on team sacks. Most fantasy leagues reward one point for each sack, providing an incremental scoring system that isn't as susceptible to randomness as points allowed.

I devised a formula to accurately project team sacks using hurries from Pro Football Focus. Hurries are a measure of how much actual pressure teams place on quarterbacks. Since sacks are quite fluky, hurries are superior even to past sacks as a way to project future sacks.

I spent some time tracking sacks and hurries for all 32 NFL teams over the past half-decade. It turns out teams' total sacks add up to around 25.0 percent of their hurries. The percentages tend to even out over the long run for entire defensive units, meaning we'd expect a team that brought down the quarterback on 35.0 percent of their hurries to regress in the following season.

From 2009 to 2011, there were 30 instances of a team sacking the quarterback on fewer than 22.0 percent of their hurries. In the following seasons, those teams registered more total sacks an amazing 73.3 percent of the time. Similarly, teams that acquired a sack on over 28.0 percent of their total hurries over that time totaled fewer sacks in the next season 76.6 percent of the time. These stats are an attempt to factor luck out of the equation when it comes to sack totals. By using hurries to gauge a team's pass rush, you can get a more accurate representation of their true talent.

So how will 2013 play out? Assuming teams' total hurries from 2012 remain stable this year, here are their most likely sack totals (based on a 25.0 percent sack rate):

1.   Chicago Bears: 48 sacks
2.   Washington Redskins: 48 sacks
3.   Cincinnati Bengals: 47 sacks
4.   San Francisco 49ers: 47 sacks

5. Minnesota Vikings: 47 sacks
6. Baltimore Ravens: 46 sacks
7. New England Patriots: 44 sacks
8. San Diego Chargers: 44 sacks
9. New Orleans Saints: 43 sacks
10. Atlanta Falcons: 43 sacks
11. Denver Broncos: 43 sacks
12. Tampa Bay Bucs: 42 sacks
13. Buffalo Bills: 42 sacks
14. Tennessee Titans: 42 sacks
15. Houston Texans: 42 sacks
16. Philadelphia Eagles: 40 sacks
17. St. Louis Rams: 40 sacks
18. New York Giants: 40 sacks
19. Seattle Seahawks: 39 sacks
20. Miami Dolphins: 39 sacks
21. Green Bay Packers: 39 sacks
22. Carolina Panthers: 38 sacks
23. Detroit Lions: 35 sacks
24. Dallas Cowboys: 35 sacks
25. Arizona Cardinals: 34 sacks
26. Cleveland Browns: 33 sacks
27. Oakland Raiders: 32 sacks
28. New York Jets: 32 sacks
29. Indianapolis Colts: 32 sacks
30. Pittsburgh Steelers: 27 sacks
31. Jacksonville Jaguars: 25 sacks
32. Kansas City Chiefs: 23 sacks

Comparing those projections to 2012 sack totals, you can see the big winners are those teams that were just unlucky last year, i.e. had a lot of hurries but not a lot of sacks. New Orleans (30), Washington (32), and New England (37) are all set to see a probable increase in team sacks in 2013. St. Louis (52) and Green Bay (47), in particular, will probably see a decline in total sack production.

It's important to note that the projections use past sacks and hurries only, taking no personnel or defensive scheme changes into account. You should factor free agent acquisitions, coaching changes, and so on into your projections. Still, it's a solid foundation from which to draft your defense. While others are drafting the Steelers because of their name, you can wait and grab the Redskins or Bengals' defense, feeling confident that they'll at least be in the top 10 in team sacks.

As a final note, I want to say if you can get away with it, don't draft a defense at all. Unless your league requires you to draft a defense, forgo one completely and draft another skill position. Then, you can wait until the week before the season to drop a player and add a defense with a favorable matchup that week.

If you absolutely must draft a defense, weigh projected team sacks heavily into your decision. Assuming you must also draft a kicker, wait until the second-last round to grab your defense. I promise you that both Washington and Cincinnati will still be on the board.

• The Bottom Line

If you don't have to draft a defense, don't do it. You can pick one up just before the season starts and then rotate them as needed based on matchups. If you're required to select a defense, do so in the second-to-last round (assuming you have to draft a kicker as well). Search for defenses with 1) a poor Week 1 opponent and 2) who figure to rack up a lot of sacks. Sack totals are one of the most consistent year-to-year stats for defenses, and you can gain value by targeting defenses that had lots of pressures in the year before, but simply got unlucky with sacks.

A Look Ahead

As I mentioned at the start, I published *How to Dominate Your Draft* in 2012, and I have a revised edition available in 2013. I also published another new book in 2013 called *How to Cash in on the Future of the Game.* Here are descriptions of both:

- *How to Cash in on the Future of the Game*

Fantasy Football for Smart People: How to Cash in on the Future of the Game is the first book of its kind to break down the actual strategies used by the top owners in the world of weekly fantasy football. With weekly fantasy football growing at an exponential rate, there's a whole lot of money to be made, and advanced weekly owners are already cashing in to the tune of hundreds of thousands of dollars in profit. With input from one of the weekly fantasy football "sharks"—FFFC $150,000 winner Peter Jennings—*How to Cash in on the Future of the Game* will show you how to manage your money, select the perfect websites, make projections, and create lineups so that you can finally treat your hobby as you always wanted—as an investment.

- *Fantasy Football for Smart People: How to Dominate Your Draft*

Fantasy Football for Smart People: How to Dominate Your Draft offers in-depth fantasy football draft strategy. The aim of the book is to provide advanced material for experienced fantasy football owners and "bottom line" analysis for novices. The book is not a collection of player rankings or projections, but rather an assessment of various draft strategies and fantasy football tenants. It will provide a solid foundation from which you can improve as an owner to dominate your draft for a decade to come.

If you liked *What the Experts Don't Want You to Know,* I promise you'll enjoy my two other titles. To prove it, I decided to publish a sample from each. Enjoy.

How to Cash in on the Future of the Game

Cha-Ching!: Money Management as the Backbone of Weekly Fantasy Football

"No matter how good you are, you're going to lose one-third of your games. No matter how bad you are, you're going to win one-third of your games. It's the other third that makes the difference." - Tommy Lasorda

If you've ever searched for fantasy football advice, the term "LOCKS" (all capital letters, usually) has become part of your vocabulary. Like the sports betting guru who offers "cant-miss" picks, many fantasy sports "experts" suggest that certain players are sure things in a given week. Calvin Johnson facing the league's 29th-ranked pass defense—you can pretty much take 150 yards and two touchdowns to the bank, right?

One of the most important steps in becoming a fantasy football master is realizing that you're going to be wrong. You're going to be wrong *a lot*. In a game filled with so much luck, your advantage over even a novice in a head-to-head weekly matchup might be, say, 2-to-1, i.e. you're still going to lose 33 percent of the time.

Since the NFL is ruled by probabilities, even a perfect fantasy owner will lose. It's vital to understand that even if you're the world's premiere fantasy owner, you're not infallible. Just as a professional poker player can lose multiple hands in a row to a novice, so too can Wally lose to Gary (and on a much more frequent basis than even most accomplished fantasy owners understand).

The same misunderstanding of probability that leads some to claim (and sometimes really believe) that their picks are fail-safe also often results in poor money management. After all, if you're wagering money as if you're a 70 percent long-term winner when you're really no better than a coin flip, that's going to lead to an empty bankroll. Thus, the percentage of your bankroll—the total amount of money with which you plan to play weekly fantasy football—that you wager on each team should be a reflection of, among other things, your expected winning percentage.

Understanding Bankroll

Since your total bankroll will be the primary factor in determining how much you can wager in a given league, it's important that the amount of money you use in your calculations is your *true* bankroll, i.e. the maximum amount of money you're *willing to lose* playing the game. If you put $1,000 into your weekly fantasy football account but plan to remove the funds if you hit a certain low point, your true bankroll is $1,000 minus your low limit. If you calculate your bets as a function of the $1,000, they'll be too high and you'll be more likely to go bankrupt. Similarly, if you plan to add more funds to your account, formulating your bets with a perceived $1,000 bankroll will potentially lead to lost profits.

There's a reason I'm kicking off this weekly fantasy football book with something that doesn't have anything at all to do with football; if your expenditures are too high, you're going to eventually lose your money. It might take a week or it might take two years, but it will happen. I really want to hammer this idea home. . .

Imagine a magical fantasy football genie has come to you and offered an enticing proposition: a guaranteed 80 percent winning percentage in weekly fantasy football. Um, sign me up. The offer comes with one caveat, though; you must bet 25 percent of your bankroll on each team, and you need to participate in a minimum of 500 leagues. Do you take the offer?

While an 80 percent winning percentage is likely unattainable over the long-run even for an expert owner, there's still no way you can take the genie's offer. Even with just a 20 percent chance of losing a game, it's going to happen. And occasionally, it will happen twice in a row. And once in a while, you'll lose three consecutive games. And, wait for it. . .over any four-game stretch (even with an incredible 80 percent expectation), you actually have a 0.16

percent chance of losing all four games—as in once in every 625 games, on average.

Would you go broke after the first four games? Probably not. But would it eventually happen? Yes. You're basically playing Russian roulette with your bankroll when, if your goal is long-term profitability, you should take chance out of the equation as much as possible. Now consider that a more realistic expected long-term winning percentage of 60 percent would result in four straight losses at *16 times the rate* of an 80 percent winning percentage, and you can see how money management starts to become the backbone of your weekly fantasy football strategy.

How much is too much?

There are all sorts of theories regarding how much of your bankroll you should spend on each game. How should your expected return affect your bet size? How about the number of players in a league? These questions haven't really been answered as it relates to weekly fantasy football.

Professional sports bettors typically wager no more than five or six percent of their bankroll on any given game, and most wagers fall under that amount. There are differences between the professional bettor and the expert fantasy owner, however. While the majority of people who fall under either label can expect a long-term winning percentage that likely falls somewhere between 55 and 60 percent, the games on which professional sports bettors place money are typically independent of one another. That is, the Sunday Bills-Jaguars matchup does nothing to affect the outcome of the Monday night Redskins-49ers game.

When fielding multiple fantasy lineups, however, the results are inherently tied to one another. You might start one player on multiple teams, for example, or you might start a quarterback and wide receiver duo. You could have the No. 1 receiver on his respective team on one of your squads and the No. 2 receiver on a different one. The dependent nature of your fantasy lineups makes them inherently volatile, i.e. it would typically be unintelligent to wager as much as you would on independent events.

On top of that, your expected winning percentage won't be 60 percent if you enter anything other than head-to-head or 50/50 leagues. If you plan to enter a 100-team league that pays out the top 10 teams, for example, you probably can't expect to win money much more than 15 to 20 percent of the time, regardless of your skills.

Your Maximum Investment: The Ultimate Formula

Whether you play weekly fantasy football for fun or for profit, you're presumably going to field more than one lineup. The number of teams you create and how you structure them—which will be a topic of later discussion—will depend on your willingness to take on risk; are you a Gary or a Wally? Nonetheless, there are some basic parameters to follow when deciding upon your optimal investment for each lineup.

In playing weekly fantasy football, I devised the following formula to determine the optimal amount to wager in each league.

- **[(Percentage of owners who won't win)/6)]*(Expected winning percentage)*(Bankroll)**

Let's take an example. Suppose your bankroll is $1,000 and you want to enter a three-team league. To determine the optimal amount to wager, you'd first need to figure out the percentage of players that wouldn't win any money in the league. In a typical three-man league, only one person wins, meaning 67 percent of the owners would lose their investment. Thus, the percentage of players who wouldn't win would be marked as "0.67." After dividing that number by 6, you'd multiply the result (0.11167) by your expected winning percentage in such a league. It is crucial that you don't overestimate your probability of winning. Actually, unless you have an established track record of success, you should estimate your chances of winning as the same as if the league were complete luck. In a three-man league, that would be 33 percent, or 0.33.

After multiplying 0.11167 by 33 percent to obtain 0.03685, you'll multiply that final number by the amount of your bankroll ($1,000). The proper amount to wager for someone in a three-team league that pays out one person is 3.685 percent, or $36.85.

Note that as you alter your expected winning percentage, the amount you should wager changes as well. If you were confident you could take down 45 percent of three-man leagues, for example, your optimum bet would increase to $50.25. Using such a method, you can change the amount you wager on your best lineups. If you participate in five head-to-head leagues and estimate your expected winning percentage to be 65 percent for the best combination of players and 55 percent for the worst, your ideal bet size with a $1,000 would gradually decline from $54.16 to $45.83.

Further, you can see how leagues with a low payout percentage subsequently lower the amount you should wager. If you're in a 100-man league that pays out just 10 percent of owners, for example, your optimal bet with a bankroll of $1,000 would shrink to only $20.00.

Depending where you play weekly fantasy football, you might be able to set your own entry fees. Most times, however, you'll be entering weekly leagues with pre-set fees, often $5, $10, $25, and so on. In general, you should go on the low end of your optimal bet calculation, i.e. if the formula says to bet $8 per game, stick with $5 leagues the majority of the time. If you have a little Gary in you, go ahead and bump it up from time to time to increase your upside.

If you play solely on sites with pre-determined entry fees and you want to be very precise about the leagues you enter and the frequency with which you bet specific dollar amounts, use the following formula to determine how you allocate funds:

- **(High-End Entry Fee – Ideal Entry Fee)/(High-End Entry Fee – Low-End Entry Fee) = Percentage of Leagues With Low-End Entry Fee**

Take your ideal entry fee (as determined by the first formula) and look up the closest dollar amounts you could wager on both the high and low ends. If your ideal bet size is $20 and the closest leagues have $25 and $10 entry fees, use the $25 league as your "High-End Entry Fee" and the $10 league as your "Low-End Entry Fee." In that example, the percentage of leagues in which you'd enter with the low-end fee would be ($25-$20)/($25-$10), or 33.3 percent, i.e. one-third of the leagues you enter should be $10 and two-thirds should be $25.

Being Flexible on Bet Sizes

In addition to your willingness to take on risk, the nature in which you formulate your weekly lineups will dictate your bet sizes. Namely, if you add the same players on multiple teams, the volatility of your bets increases. If you theoretically used the same lineup for every team and wagered 25 percent of your bankroll, for example, a very poor week could legitimately leave you with no returns for the week, depending on your league structure. On the flip side, if your player selection is very diverse, i.e. the same players aren't on multiple teams, you can increase the amount you place on each squad. The above formulas can provide you with a strong baseline from which to work, but the exact amounts you wager on each lineup should be molded according to a variety of factors.

I'll talk more about player selection in subsequent chapters, but it's important to know that it goes hand-in-hand with the size of your wagers. Remember, your goal as a fantasy owner is to increase upside without significantly increasing risk. Thus, the relationship between player selection and bet sizes should be an inverse one; the more you diversify your lineups to limit downside, the more money you can place on each team to subsequently improve your upside.

In the Bonus

There's no easier method by which you can accrue profit while playing weekly fantasy football than by unlocking bonuses when you deposit money. Take advantage. Some sites offer ridiculous bonuses on your first deposit and that can turn into a hefty sum of cash if you play your cards right. The big initial bonus offered by most weekly fantasy sports sites is a major reason to deposit your whole bankroll right from the start. If you say to yourself, "I'll deposit $1,000 now and $1,000 later," you could be missing out on a sizeable amount of bonus money. You'll need to earn your bonus by participating in leagues, but as long as your money management on point, you should have no trouble unlocking the entire initial deposit bonus.

Can proper money management lead to long-term winnings?

When you participate in weekly fantasy football, you don't get to do it for free. The sites obviously need to profit, so they take out what's known as "juice" or "the rake"—the percentage of total money that doesn't go back into the pockets of owners. The rake is calculated by simply subtracting the total payouts from the total money wagered, then dividing by the total money wagered. If you're in a 10-team league with a $100 entry fee and the site pays out $900, for example, the juice is (1,000 − 900)/1,000 = 0.1, or 10 percent. I'll return to the rake in a bit, but it should be the first aspect of any league you examine prior to entering. Juice might be delicious in the real world, but not so much in the realm of weekly fantasy football.

The question is whether or not weekly fantasy owners can overcome the juice to make money. The industry standard rake for weekly fantasy football is 10 percent, but it can be as high as 12 percent or as low as nothing in big-money leagues. Typically, it's somewhere around the 9.1 percent juice charged by sportsbooks on standard 11-to-10 bets.

So if weekly fantasy sites pay out around the same amount as sportsbooks and only a handful of people in the world can make money betting on sports over the long-run, does my Uncle Bruce who sets his fantasy lineups in his boxers while he's eating homemade beef jerky have any chance at profitability? The answer isn't much different than it is for sports betting; most people are going to lose their money in the long-term, but some can win. Actually, it's easier to win weekly fantasy football than it is to bet on sports, despite potentially reduced payouts. Here's why. . .

Weekly Fantasy Sports vs. Sports Betting

There's a pretty widespread perception that when a sportsbook sets lines, it does so based on public opinion. That is, they care less about how the game will turn out and more about taking in even money on each side of every game. That's not actually true, however.

At one time when sports bettors were pretty square as a whole, sportsbooks could get away with setting a line based entirely on public perception simply because there were very few wise guys who could beat those lines. In a world filled with analytics and in-depth stat analysis, though, the average sports bettor has improved. A lot. Now when the brilliant minds in Vegas set lines, they do so primarily based on reality; if they set a weak line, wise guys will quickly exploit it and the squares will follow. Thus, the nature of sports betting has changed. Vegas might post a weak line now and again, but for the most part, their lines properly reflect the quality of the participating teams, meaning you have to outsmart them to win.

What that means is that the average sports bettor is no longer betting against the general public as he once was. Sure, there are elements of perception inherent to every line, but these days bettors are basically going up against Vegas—their data heads and advanced computers included. Only the cream of the crop—which probably isn't you, sorry—can make a living betting on sports.

Along with the boom in popularity of fantasy sports has come the return of betting against the general public. When you play weekly fantasy football, you don't need to outsmart a professional statistician, but rather Joe Dillard from Billings, Montana who has four kids and a pet iguana named Lester, just lost his job at T.G.I. Friday's, and puts 20 percent of his bankroll on each team. Yeah, go ahead and give me Joe. ***If Joe is really out there and decides to buy my book, that's going to be a *super* awkward e-mail exchange.***

Ultimately, the fact that weekly fantasy football allows you to compete against other owners makes the reduced payouts worth the hassle. Again, most owners still won't be able to overcome the 10 percent juice, but some will. As it relates to long-term investment strategies, wise guys—Wallys—can truly make a living playing weekly fantasy football. You aren't going to be able to sustain long-term profits without astute money management.

Reduce the Juice

Regardless of the exact payout, you want to reduce the amount of juice taken in each league. A site that takes out 12 percent of all league entry fees and one that removes eight percent might not sound all that different, but let's do the math. . .

Assume you participate in head-to-head leagues with $100 entry fees. One league pays out $176 to the winner and the other is $184. Who cares about a measly eight bucks, right? Well, imagine you enter 15 such leagues per week over the course of a 17-

week season—255 total leagues. With a stout 60 percent winning rate, you'll take down 153 leagues and lose 102 of them. On the site with the reduced eight percent juice, you'll bring in $12,852 and lose $10,200 for a net profit of $2,652.

Playing out the same scenario on the site that takes a hefty 12 percent commission, however, would net you a total profit of just $1,428—a difference of $1,224 (nearly 50 percent) over the course of the year. More important, to make as much cash on the site with the higher juice, you'd need to win 61.7 percent of those 255 leagues instead of an even 60 percent, and that 1.7 percent jump is a bigger one than you think.

How big? Take a look at this passage in an article at RotoGrinders.com:

> At a standard 10% rake you would need to win 55.6% of your HU leagues to break even. For the sake of this post, I am going to assume that 4% of all players can beat a 55.6% rake long-term. The percentage of winning players in online poker is known to be around 10%, and it is also known that the percentage is lower than that for daily fantasy sports. For a 10% rake with 4% beating it you get the following distribution:

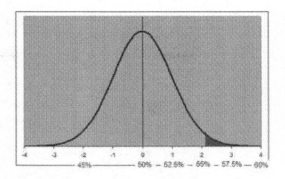

The red area of the curve indicates the winning players, and the gray area under the curve indicates the losing players. Now let's say that you lowered the rake to 7.5% for a 25% rake reduction from 10%. You would get the following curve.

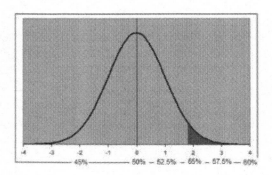

As you can see, you have more than doubled the number of winning players by reducing the rake by 25% as now you only need to *win 54% of your leagues to break even. As the rake gets lowered you capture more and more players into the "winning" area of the curve. This is the power of the normal distribution. Our rake goes down to 6% which requires a 53.2% winning rate to beat long-term. Below is what that would look like.*

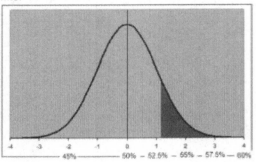

Now we are talking! The move from 7.5% to 6% more than doubled the number of players that can be long-term profitable. Going to the extreme of 0% rake would allow 50% of players to be long-term profitable.

Unless you have some screws loose, reduce the juice. Moose.

Other Perks

Juice is important, but you don't necessarily need to be confined to the site or two that collect the lowest rake. Different sites offer different perks, and sometimes things like higher bonuses can make up for increased juice. Plus, in the same way that sports bettors shop around for the best lines, you too should shop around for the best player prices. If you really love Robert Griffin III in a given week, you might be able to put up with a slightly higher juice from one site if RGIII's salary (in terms of the percentage of the total cap) is much lower than anywhere else.

Similarly, sites weight each position differently. One might have the top quarterback salary as 16 percent of the total salary cap when another has the same guy at 19 percent, so you should rank players based on the percentage of your salary cap they exhaust. If Site X offers 90.9 percent payouts but has the quarterback you covet at 16 percent of the overall cap and Site Y offers 91.5 percent payouts but has the same quarterback at 22 percent of the total cap, you might want to take the reduced payout from Site X in order to optimize your lineup and ultimately increase your winning percentage.

A Cautionary Tale

Every season, I pick the winner and score of every NFL game. Over the past three seasons, I've compiled a record of 510-257-1 straight up, 405-337-

26 against the spread, and 402-349-17 on totals. If you placed $1,100 on every game using my recommendations, you would have won $52,400.

Of course, that assumes you have an unlimited (or very high) bankroll. Though I've demonstrated a decent long-term winning percentage on NFL bets, I go through losing streaks like everyone else. Actually, although I finished the 2012 season with a 135-114-7 record against the spread, I began the season horrendously. I was 4-12 after Week 1 and 8-23-1 after Week 2. Through Week 6, I was barely staying afloat at 36-53. It wasn't until after Week 13 that I even hit .500 on the season! It took a ridiculous 52-26-1 record over the final five weeks of the season for me to even approach my long-term winning percentage.

The point is that no matter how much you know football, placing an exorbitantly high percentage of your bankroll on each wager simply can't be sustained. When the difference between a professional bettor and a coin flip is often just five percentage points, the most important aspect of profiting from betting—or weekly fantasy football— is effective money management.

To appropriately understand the dangers of poor money management, imagine that Gary began following my picks during Week 13 of the 2012 season. He would have thought I was a savant, hitting on nearly 70 percent of my picks over a decent sample size 79 games. Gary wants a piece of that pie, so he decides that he's going to use my knowledge to start the 2013 season. And he's so confident in my system that he decides that he's going to wager $1,100 of his $10,000 bankroll on each game—11.1 percent. Had he done that at the end of the 2012 season, he would have profited $23,400 in only five weeks. Cha-ching.

Except there's one small problem. Instead of continuing my hot streak to start the 2013 season, imagine that it begins as the 2012 season did. After Week 1, I'm 4-12. Guess what? Gary just lost $9,200—92 percent of his money. With a bet size that was too high—but not unheard of from novices—Gary basically went broke in a single week.

The 10 Laws of Money Management

If you want to play weekly fantasy football—and you want to play it for more than a few weeks before going bankrupt—you absolutely must have a sound financial plan. It doesn't have to be complex, but if you're consistently placing 11 percent of your total bankroll on each matchup, you're going to lose your money.

Law No. 1: You will not believe in "sure things."

Weekly fantasy football is a game ruled by probability. You might be a quality owner—say, a 60

percent long-term winner in head-to-head leagues—
and you'll still lose all of your money if you're playing
as if you're an 80 percent long-term winner. There
are no sure things, and you have to understand the
percentages in order to profit from weekly fantasy
football.

**Law No. 2: You will not wager more than you can
afford to lose.**

Your bankroll is the total amount of money you're
willing to *lose*. If you place $1,000 into an account
but plan to remove the money if you dip down
below $500, your bet sizes—based on a $1,000
bankroll—will be too large in relation to your actual
bankroll of $500.

**Law No. 3: You will bet a percentage of your
bankroll that resembles the result of this formula:
[(Percentage of owners who won't
win)/6)]*(Expected winning percentage)*(Bankroll)**

Your bet sizes should be flexible based on a variety
of factors, but this formula can provide you with a
useful baseline.

**Law No. 4: You will seek bonuses whenever
possible.**

You can greatly enhance your bankroll—especially if
you're new to weekly fantasy football—by taking
advantage of deposit and reload bonuses. Similarly,

look for any opportunities for free money, such as freerolls (which I'll discuss in the next chapter).

Law No. 5: You will reduce the juice whenever possible.

There are lots of ways to maximize your profits when playing weekly fantasy football—searching for bonuses, tweaking your lineups to increase your expected winning percentage, seeking out weak opponents—but the easiest is to minimize the amount of money you "pay" for playing, i.e. the rake given to the site. When analyzing each site or particular matchup to enter, the first thing you should do is calculate the cost to play.

Law No. 6: You will play weekly fantasy football on multiple sites.

There are a variety of benefits to playing on numerous sites, including maximizing your bonuses and benefiting from all of the perks each site has to offer. You can even search for the cheapest prices for your favorite players in a given week, using specific players on particular sites where they don't eat up too much of your cap space.

Law No. 7: You will not wager more on "hot streaks."

When I finished the 2012 season on a roll, I wasn't really "hot" in that I was picking games better; I used the exact same methodology that led to my horrible start to the season. In effect, I was just lucky. You're going to go through hot streaks and cold spells, but don't let those significantly affect your wagers. Not only will that not lead to long-term profitability, but it will actually increase your chances of going bankrupt.

Law No. 8: You will understand the difference between weekly fantasy football and sports betting.

While there are obvious similarities between weekly fantasy football and sports betting, the primary difference between the two is that the former pits owners against one another. That means that instead of competing against a sportsbook filled with math geniuses who rarely mess up a line, you're competing against a wide range of other fantasy football owners, many of whom are just like you. That allows for long-term profitability for more than just a handful of sophisticated bettors.

Law No. 9: You will know your long-term winning percentage.

You simply cannot properly manage your bankroll without some sort of idea of your long-term winning percentage. If you don't have a track history of weekly fantasy football league results, you should estimate your winning percentage to be nothing more than totally random, i.e. 50 percent in a head-to-head league, 33 percent in a three-team league, and so on.

Law No. 10: You will maximize upside and minimize risk.

You don't need to seek upside at all costs, nor do you need to always minimize your risk. But you need to do at least one of them. If you're playing with one lineup—an inherently risky decision—you need to diversify your league selection so that you don't have too much money riding on one outcome. The amount of risk you're willing to take on should be a reflection of your bankroll, your expected winning percentage, and your overall goals.

How to Dominate Your Draft

Identifying Value: Regression, Randomness, and Running Backs

Back in 2008, I had running back Thomas Jones ranked well ahead of most owners. Jones was playing for the Jets and coming off a season in which he ran for 1,119 yards, but averaged just 3.6 yards-per-rush and scored only two total touchdowns. Those two scores represented just 0.59 percent of Jones' 338 touches in 2007.

ESPN had Jones ranked 21st among all running backs. I had him 10th. Why would I possibly rank a then 30-year old running back coming off a season in which he tallied 3.6 yards-per-carry and two total touchdowns in my top 10? Regression toward the mean.

Regression toward the mean is a phenomenon wherein "extreme" results tend to end up closer to the average on subsequent measurements. That is, a running back who garners 338 touches and scores only twice is far more likely to improve upon that performance than one who scored 25 touchdowns.

0-16 Detroit Lions: A Coach's Dream?

Regression toward the mean is the reason the NFL coaches who take over the worst teams are in a far superior position to those who take over quality squads. If I were an NFL coach, there is no team I would prefer to take over more than the 2008 Detroit Lions. Coming off an 0-16 season, the Lions were almost assured improvement in 2009 simply because everything went wrong the previous season. Even though Detroit was a bad team, any coach who took over in 2009 was basically guaranteed to oversee improvement in following years.

The same sort of logic is the reason that there are so many first-round "busts" in fantasy football. Players almost always get selected in the first round because they had monster years in the prior season. In effect, most first-rounders are the "outliers" from the prior season's data, and their play is more likely to regress than improve in the current year. It isn't that those players are poor picks, but rather that the combination of quality play, health, and other random factors that led to their prior success is unlikely to work out so fortunately again.

Players Aren't "Due"

Walk into any casino in America and you will see lines of hopeful grandmothers lining up behind slot machines that haven't paid recently. Since the machines pay a specific average of money over the course of their lives and those numbers always even out over the long run, surely an underperforming slot machine must be due to pay out soon, right?

This is one of the biggest misconceptions regarding statistics and regression, and it is the cause of millions of lost dollars each year. In a set of random data, previous occurrences have absolutely no effect on future events. If you flip a coin right now and it lands on heads, the probability that it lands on heads again on your next flip is still 50 percent.

Similarly, if the overall payout rate of a slot machine is 40 percent, the most likely outcome of placing $1,000 into it is walking away with $400. You could walk away big or you (theoretically) could lose every penny, but the most probable single dollar amount you could "win" is $400. So when the previous 100 pulls of the lever are fruitless, the payout "improvement" that is likely to take place over the next 100 pulls isn't because the machine is "due," but rather it is simply working as normal. That is regression toward the mean.

But football isn't random.

Football isn't totally random, but it's more random than you think. Actually, some statisticians have estimated the "luck factor" to be as high as .924 in the NFL. That means on any given week, the "true" winning percentage of teams that win is really around .538. In a league in which only 16 games make up a season, the talent gap between teams is lessening, and turnovers play a huge role in wins, the amount of luck involved in the game is more so than any other professional sport.

Even disregarding the potential randomness of NFL outcomes, the identification of underperforming players can be of incredible value to fantasy owners. As it relates to Thomas Jones, it doesn't really matter how much randomness was involved in his two-touchdown season. Heading into the 2008 season as the workhorse back on a team with a strong offensive line and no real reason to think he was a fundamentally poor short-yardage runner, projecting Jones to score more than a handful of times was easy. I projected him at 10 touchdowns. He scored 15.

So when other owners are jumping all over the players who had "extreme" seasons the prior year, look for talented players who actually underperformed. As long as they get similar opportunities to make plays, their numbers will probably improve. For fantasy owners, that represents value.

Of course that doesn't mean you should select weaker players simply because they had poor years. In the first few rounds, you are almost certain to draft outliers who played better than normal the season before. Your job is to recognize which players' value is *primarily* the result of random factors, and thus likely to regress to the average, and which is based largely on talent, and thus likely to repeat itself.

How To Determine an "Average" Season

Of course, not every player has the same "average" season. If we were to simulate 1,000 NFL seasons, Ray Rice's per-season totals would obviously eclipse those of, say, Beanie Wells. So recognizing how players' stats will regress involves identifying (or at least intelligently estimating) their "average" season. In a typical season, how many more yards, touchdowns, and receptions will Rice score as compared to Wells? Until we establish mean seasons for each player, we have no base from which we can determine to where their numbers from the previous season will regress. That is, the totals for Rice and Wells aren't likely to regress to the mean for all backs, but rather they will regress to their specific averages.

Determining that value can be tricky. One of the easiest ways is to determine how many "lucky" plays a player benefited from in a specific year. We have already seen that stats like interceptions are inherently fluky, and thus very likely to regress to the mean in subsequent seasons. Aaron Rodgers is a heck of a player, but he's very unlikely to ever again match his 45:6 TD-to-INT ratio from 2011.

Other statistics, such as touchdowns and long-yardage plays, are not necessarily extremely random, but they can still have a major impact on fantasy scores. In Chris Johnson's 2009 season in which he broke the record for total yards from scrimmage, he totaled seven touchdowns of 50-plus yards. That number is the ninth best of all-time. . .for a career!

Despite possessing game-breaking speed, it would have been foolish to believe Johnson would repeat his 2009 campaign. Our job as fantasy owners was to determine what an "average" Johnson season would look like, taking the extent of Johnson's 2009 "luck" into account.

Still, the task of predicting average seasons on an individual basis is a difficult one. There is no single method to do it, but understanding the inherent instability of interceptions, fumbles, long touchdowns, field goals, etc. is a start.

The Myth of Overworked Running Backs

One of the most frequent mistakes made by fantasy football owners is assuming all correlations are due to a causal effect. Lots of things in life are related, yet have no effect on one another. The old notion that great running teams win football games is an illusion based on a misunderstanding of the correlation/causation distinction, for example. Yes, winning teams average more rushing yards than losing teams, but that's because teams that are *already winning* run the ball late in games. In reality, they usually gain the lead by passing the football effectively.

A prevalent fantasy football "truism" is the idea that overworked running backs struggle in subsequent seasons. There are numerous studies out there detailing how running backs struggle when coming off a season with 350 touches, or 370 touches, or however many touches is necessary for the study to make sense. The exact number is usually chosen ex post facto and is to be regarded as a "magical threshold" that spells doom in the following season if crossed.

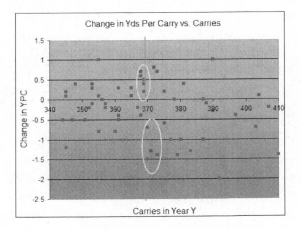

In a study on the effect of 370-plus carries on running backs, the number seems to be chosen after the fact because it makes the numbers more extreme. You can see the abundance of running backs that actually improved their yards-per-carry, yet came just a few carries short of 370. Are we really to believe a running back who carried the ball

365 times in a season is to be trusted in the subsequent season, but those with 370 carries are doomed?

In reality, though, running backs who garner a large number of touches in a season are generally more likely to see a drop in production and health in the following year, but that information is both insignificant and irrelevant.

Think about what it takes to acquire nearly 400 touches in a season. For one, a running back needs to be healthy. Really healthy. Secondly, chances are he is running efficiently. Running backs who average 3.5 yards-per-carry over the first half of the season don't generally continue to see the 24 carries a game needed to break the 370 threshold. Thus, our sample size of high-carry backs is skewed by those performing well.

That's where regression toward the mean comes in. By filtering out injured and underperforming backs, selecting those with a high number of carries means we are selecting the outliers in more areas than one. We aren't isolating the numbers based on carries, but rather based on health and efficiency as well. So when we make conclusions concerning health and efficiency, all we're really saying is players who have unusual health and a higher-than-normal YPC are likely to have worse health and a lower YPC the following year. Uh, yeah. . .no shit.

So yeah, running backs with a lot of carries in year Y usually see a drop in production in year+1, but it's a product of regression, not a heavy workload.

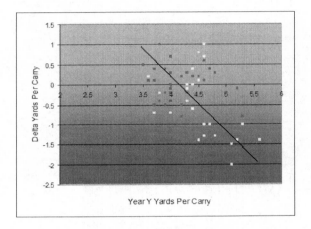

The efficiency of *all* running backs tends to regress to the mean, not just those coming off seasons with heavy workloads. If a back runs for 6.0 YPC in a year, he will probably see a decline in efficiency whether he had 50 carries or 400.

Thus, while the production of a running back coming off a season with a heavy workload is likely to decrease, it is not a legitimate reason to avoid that player in fantasy drafts. The (probable) decrease in production is due to the previous season being a statistical outlier (a result that is unusually far from the mean).

The best way to look at the situation is this: what is the running back's chance of generating production that is comparable to the previous year? It is actually *the same* as it was prior to the start of the previous season, i.e. the workload has no noticeable effect on his ability to produce.

For example, if a running back has a 20 percent chance of garnering 2,000 total yards in a season, that percentage remains stable (assuming his skill level and supporting cast do the same) from year to year. Thus, the probability of the player following a 2,000 yard season with another is unlikely, but not due to a heavy workload (a necessity for such productive output), but rather the fact that he only had a 20 percent chance to do so from the start. We wrongly (and ironically) attribute the decrease in production to the player's prior success when, in reality, no such causal relationship exists.

How to Predict Running Backs' Yards-Per-Carry

As I wrote earlier, fantasy owners need to determine which aspects of players' games are repeatable, and which are a matter of luck. Understanding the position consistency I detailed in previous sections is a start, and it gives us a foundation from which we can make projections of specific statistics.

Regression toward the mean is a factor in all projections. Rather than simply arbitrarily guessing projections, there are formulas we can use to make more educated predictions (albeit still "guesses"). To exemplify the magnitude of regression in projections, let's examine how to go about predicting a running back's yards-per-carry.

It turns out yards-per-carry has a correlational strength of about 0.43 from season to season. That number is similar to the 0.50 correlational strength we saw with year-to-year rushing yards-per-game. It also means a large aspect of predicting running backs' YPC is simply accounting for the "luck" they experienced the season before.

After all is said and done, we can accurately predict YPC with the following formula:

$YPC\_n+1 = LgAvgYPC - 0.04 + 0.43*(YrNDiff)$

In layman's terms, the most accurate YPC projection we can make is taking 3/7 of the previous year's YPC and adding it to 4/7 of the league average (about 4.2), then subtracting 0.04. For a running back who averaged 6.0 yards-per-carry, the projection would be 6.0 (3/7) + 4.2 (4/7) − 0.04 = 4.93 YPC.

Notice the formula will decrease the projected YPC of any back who registered above 4.2, but increase the YPC of anyone below that figure. A back who mustered only 3.8 YPC in year Y is most likely to total 3.8 (3/7) + 4.2 (4/7) − 0.04 = 3.99 YPC in year Y+1.

223 | P a g e

There will be more information on projecting specific stats for each position in following analysis. A lot of that will be based on regression toward the mean, but there are certainly a lot of other factors at play. It is important to remember these formulas aren't a definitive source for final projections, but rather a solid base from which to work.

The Bottom Line
- Regression to the mean states "extreme" events tend to regress toward the average, and fantasy owners can use it to acquire value. Just as traders buy low and sell high, fantasy owners can pinpoint which players are due for boosts or declines in production based on how much of their previous production was caused by random factors.

- Your job as an owner isn't to select players who had poor seasons, but rather those who are being undervalued due to production that was below their "average season." In effect, you are buying low on players whose value will "regress" upward.

- Regression toward the mean shows us running backs coming off seasons with heavy workloads are likely to see a decline in production, but not because of the workload itself. Instead, those backs are necessarily the outliers from the previous season, and statistically likely to regress. In practical terms, it means there's no reason for owners to purposely avoid running backs who had a lot of touches the prior season.

- One of the easiest and most accurate ways to predict a running back's yards-per-carry is to multiply his YPC from the previous year by 3/7, then add that number to 4/7 of the league average YPC (which works out to 2.4), then subtract 0.04. Other factors are of course relevant, but this is a great foundation from which to work.

That's all folks. Remember to check out *How to Dominate Your Draft* and *How to Cash in on the Future of the Game*. You can also head over to FantasyFootballDrafting.com for my customized 2013 rankings and draft guide. Thanks for reading.

Special thanks to:

RotoWire, FF Today, Fifth Down Blog, and rotoViz: All leaders in terms of providing unique, useful fantasy content, these sites allowed me to publish various articles prior to, during, and after the process of writing *What the Experts Don't Want You to Know.*

Made in the USA
Lexington, KY
19 November 2015